10.14

D0108617

Underground Notes

Underground Notes
By
Mihajlo Mihajlov

Introduction by Vladimir Maximov

Translated by Maria Mihajlov Ivusic
and Christopher W. Ivusic

SHEED ANDREWS and MC MEEL, INC.
SUBSIDIARY OF UNIVERSAL PRESS SYNDICATE
KANSAS CITY

Library of Congress Cataloging in Publication Data

Mihajlov, Mihajlo, 1934-
    Underground notes.

    Bibliography: p.
      1. Russia — Intellectual life — 1970 -   —Addresses, essays, lectures. 2. Communism — Russia — Addresses, essays, lectures. I. Title.
DK276.M483   947.085   76-21772
ISBN 0-8362-0652-5

Contents

Preface

This collection contains my articles on the theme of religious renaissance, the first rays of which one can presently observe in Russia and Eastern Europe. All the articles, except one, were written within the last three years.

For many people, the religious renaissance is a puzzling and incomprehensible phenomenon, because of the spirit of our scientific-technical era. It is also paradoxical that the language of the new religious consciousness, which I call "planetary" consciousness, has almost nothing to do with the language used up to this day by all churches and religious movements. But the very word "religion" means "link"—the link of the inner world of man with the outside world, with the whole cosmos, and most of all, with the Creator. This is why, when people claim that there is a definite link between the inner world of man (his faith, his hope, and his love) and the actual destiny of each man, what they are talking about is religious consciousness, although the language they use to grasp the existence of that link is the language of science ("laws").

Of course, that link has nothing in common with that mechanical influence of the inner world of man on the events of his life, an influence claimed by the psychoanalysts—not only Freud, but also Jung. On the contrary, the new consciousness directly rejects every mechanical link and insists only on the dependency, inexplicable to us, but nevertheless fully real, of the whole outside world on the world within us. This dependency manifests itself not only in the personal life of an individual, but also in *life itself* and in history.

For the contemporary man who is convinced that he is just a blade of grass, totally under the power of physical, biological, psychical, social, and other laws the basic claims of the new consciousness are, of course, completely incomprehensible. They might seem to him as nonsensical as a claim today that the earth does not revolve around the sun, but vice versa; that Ptolemy was right and Copernicus wrong. Thus, for many, many people the coming religious renaissance will be unacceptable. But its acceptance does not depend on will. The awareness of the outer world's dependency on the inner world bursts imperiously into the human spirit, despite one's wishes and established scientific and nonscientific opinions. It comes only through personal experience, and most often by suffering, which destroys all our convictions that something else in the world is to blame for our destiny (social system, nature, disease, "accident").

That is why the first shoots of the new religious consciousness appeared where the unbearable pressure of the outside totalitarian world on the human being was the most terrible. And that means in Russia. However, this religious rebirth has meaning and importance for all mankind, owing to the industrial-technological culture that has already become planetary. That culture is based on *the dogma* that the laws governing the cosmos do not depend on our inner world, let alone on our passions, hopes, and desires. That dogma further maintains that the world, nature, and cosmos are not connected with us and that we can therefore exploit the outer world-object to the maximum degree. Of course, the exploitation depends wholly on our reason, science, and technology, all of which recognize the laws of the external world. It is assumed that neither the external world nor man could escape the power of these laws.

When man starts looking at the world as an object, and not as *a living entity,* linked in some mysterious way with his soul, then all his fellow men gradually become objects, so that man comes finally to feel completely alone. He finds himself in total loneliness in the cosmos-object. Yet the suffering brought about by the loneliness clears the way for the religious rebirth which, in turn, makes the world again a living entity. Man starts to realize that he's fully responsible for the destiny of that living entity, and thus his soul leaves its solitary confinement.

The new awareness is not easy to come to. The human spirit has been for too long polluted with false ideas and theories about the power of human reason and science. I substantiate this claim in my polemics with Milovan Djilas, a man of rare courage and great intellect (despite his unseemly past and his membership in the inhuman organization) who shares my political opinions, and whose friend I am honored and privileged to be.

It is too early to talk about the unavoidable conclusions to which the new "planetary" consciousness will lead. These conclusions would undoubtedly terribly frighten the people who have not yet reached the boundaries where the dogma about the world-objects starts to crumble. But the time for that will come, too.

Some articles of this book have already been published in English, in a somewhat shortened form, in different newspapers, magazines, most often in the *New York Times*. Some have also appeared in other languages (Russian, Italian, Finnish, Swedish, etc.). Only one article appeared in Yugoslavia — and that was ten years ago, when it was still possible for me to publish in the press of the country in which I live.

The fact that I am able to write and publish my thoughts at all, at least abroad (despite the court ban on my writing and public statements, the impossibility of traveling freely abroad, and the almost regular badgering in the Yugoslav press) is entirely due to the support of world public opinion, that invisible but very real spiritual connection which Solzhenitsyn mentioned in his Nobel Prize speech.

In this sense, the support which I have had the honor and

privilege to receive from Mr. James Andrews, who is editor of Universal Press Syndicate, and who was kind enough to even try to accredit me officially as a correspondent of U.P.S. in Belgrade, is of paramount importance to me. I am therefore very happy that this collection of articles dedicated to the theme which stirs me most is being made available for reading to his fellow-Americans by Mr. Andrews.

Mihajlo Mihajlov

Novi Sad, Yugoslavia

Introduction

His spiritual ascent was impetuous and almost vertical. From *Moscow Summer* to "Mystical Experiences of the Labor Camps," there is a distance of enormous life dimension. Reviewing the list of Mihajlo Mihajlov's works of only the last five years, one is astounded at his great capacity for work, the diversity of his interests, the scope of his view so inherent to his wholeness, and more specifically, the purposefulness of his spiritual search. More than forty articles, studies, and essays have appeared in the most diversified vehicles of the world press, from the *New York Times* to Possev Publishing House, all during a span of little more than four years, under conditions of the most inventive legal and illegal prosecution!

Having begun, one should add, as did many of his generation, with a legitimate criticism of some facets of the socialist system in its existing state, and having undergone an agonizing opposition within himself, he arrived at a religious insight and a categorical rejection of totalitarian forms of Marxism in general. One can imagine the toll this took on a person of such purity of heart and such principles as Mihajlov!

For us—Russians—his intense and exacting interest specifically in the culture of our motherland, its problems and confrontations together with its failures and achievements, is doubly dear. Mihajlov was one of the first to respond to the works of a remarkable Russian writer of the younger generation—Andrei Synavsky-Abram Tertz. Brilliant and deep analyses of the first books of this great master in *Flight from the Test Tube* will forever remain a notable landmark in the history of contemporary thought. In his articles about L. Tolstoy, L. Andreev, A. Remizov, L. Shestov, E. Zamjatin, B. Pasternak, E. Shvarts, and A. Solzhenitsyn, Mihajlov revealed

Translated by Alexey A. Kiselev.

himself to be not only a first-rate literary scholar, but also a profound philosopher, masterfully erecting before us unbegotten for an ordinary eye the "ties of time" and reason of reasons of numerous events of our epoch.

One may agree or disagree with his endeavor to reconcile Christianity with socialism (attempts by his forerunners in this direction have been fruitless to this day); however, unlike some religious opportunists of our time, who cleverly conjoined their Christian beliefs with political adaptation, Mihajlo Mihajlov pays for his search with the ultimate price of personal sacrifice and detachment. In him, in his fight and spiritual passion, in our days, before our very eyes, is the embodiment of the heavenly spirit of the passionate early Christians.

Mihajlo Mihajlov was with us—the representatives of the new Russian literature and democratic movement, from its very first days and we, in response, consider it our duty to declare to him our direct and unwavering solidarity with his fate and his work.

Precisely because of this, I consider it an honor to write this short introduction for Mihajlo Mihajlov's remarkable book and to wish it a great impact and (of which I am absolutely certain) a long life.

Vladimir Maximov

Paris, France
October 1975

Introduction

Two Convergences

The word "convergence" has become fashionable. Since 1968, when the well-known theses of the Soviet academician Sakharov appeared, polemics about the so-called convergence of the two systems have not ceased. This is understandable, although the idea itself is not new. The importance of this writing by a scientist critical toward authority is impossible to overestimate. Under the conditions of world tension the free voice of the Soviet academician aroused great hopes of possibilities and ways for democratization in the Soviet Union. Besides, this appearance was the first indication of the political activization of the Soviet scientific and technical intelligentsia.

Reactionary persons in the USSR gave the theory of convergence a hostile reception. A similar reaction can be observed among the Western conservatives. In essence, both regard convergence as a roundabout way for the adversary to subvert the existing system. The idea of convergence formulated by Academician Sakharov finds its support generally in the liberal milieu, and particularly among scientific-technical intelligentsia of both systems.

It seems to me that the controversy is beside the point. The issue is not whether convergence will occur or not, but *what kind* will it be. I think that our civilization is at a crossroads from which either roads would lead toward convergence; but one I would call positive and the other negative convergence. And it seems to me that Sakharov and many others who sympathize with the idea of convergence are not aware of the possibility of negative convergence.

The argument of Sakharov and his followers is particularly technocratic. To avoid a nuclear world catastrophe, to control the population explosion, and to solve the problem of food, a world government is necessary. This can be brought about if the social contradictions in the capitalist countries are smoothed over by the introduction of socialist elements in society, and if, in socialist countries, political democratization enables scientists and technical intelligentsia to take the place of party bureaucrats. In short, for the salvation of mankind, a rapprochement of the two systems is necessary, and it will result from the development of both in the direction of a peculiar democratic socialism. That is what Sakharov calls it—"socialist convergence."

The condition for such a development is primarily liberalization or even liquidation of the one-party dictatorship in the USSR. This, according to Sakharov, must be engendered by the requirements of the scientific-technical revolution.

It seems to me that inherent in this argument are the basic shortcomings of the technocratic way of thinking: On the one hand, the democratization of society in totalitarian countries is the basic condition for scientific-technical progress and convergence. On the other hand, this very scientific-technical progress supposedly leads toward a democratic society of planetary dimensions.

But a very great question remains: To what extent is scientific-technical progress tied to the realization of freedom? One might conditionally agree that scientific-technical backwardness makes it difficult to create a free society. But to say that the high degree of scientific-technical development in itself ensures freedom is quite impossible. We don't have to go far for examples. Hitler's Germany is a wonderful model of a scientifically-technical highly developed totalitarian society.

The elimination of conflicts between totalitarian society and scientific-industrial revolution is a realizable, technical matter, that in no way affects the foundations of totalitarianism. Why delude ourselves? Scientific-technical progress and even convergence on this route do not guarantee freedom. Freedom of men and society is not a scientific-technical problem, but an existential one. That means *first of all a religious problem.* The elimination of the obstacles to the development of a scientific-technical revolution in the USSR, with which Sakharov is concerned, is possible by substitution of a technocracy for the party bureaucracy now existing. Not much freedom would be gained in such circumstances, yet this way of development seems to Sakharov the most suitable. He foresees the liquidation of the one-party system only if the party refuses "to bring about leadership by scientific-democratic method, which is historically necessary."

As a scientist, Sakharov knows very well the dangers of scientific progress in the weapons which science puts into the hands of the powers-that-be. But where is the guarantee that technocracy will not use science to suppress freedom in the same way the party bureaucracy has done? There is no guarantee. It is only in the conscience of the scientist. And conscience can, but does not have to be, in harmony with science.

And since the goal is progress, then freedom—political, religious, etc.—is only a means which today is both necessary and important, but tomorrow may become a hindrance. Is Sakharov going to renounce freedom if it suddenly becomes an obstacle on the road to scientific development? This is not an academic question; after all, the "Sharashka," the concentration camp laboratories for scientists described by Solzhenitsyn in the *First Circle,* under somewhat improved organization, could very well develop science and technology. It is not difficult to organize a free exchange of scientific information even without the introduction of a free press.

If the goal is scientific-technical progress, and freedom is only a means, then it is not difficult to imagine the convergence of the two systems as a *mixture* of the societies depicted by Orwell in *1984* and by Huxley in *Brave New World.* And that is the possibility of a negative convergence, which, among other things, does not exclude the possibility of wars. The more Stalin's USSR and Hitler's Germany became similar (converged), the more unavoidable became the clash between them. If China were presently on the scientific-technical level of the USSR, we would not have to wait long for a war.

But another convergence, a positive one, is possible: a convergence which leads toward a universal society, truly bringing peoples closer, because not science and technology but freedom alone brings us together, and only a free mankind can avoid a nuclear war. Such a convergence is conditioned mainly by the question of freedom, not on a plane of scientific, technical progress, but on an existential, religious plane. The connection between freedom and religion is not so obvious to the people in the West. In totalitarian societies where a man's true impulse toward freedom leads to the concentration camp or the psychiatric hospital, the link between freedom and religion fully manifests itself. *Only when* man feels that by submitting to oppression he is losing his soul, his "I," himself forever—and that this loss is worse than any physical torture or even death—*only then* can man rise against totalitarian dictatorship. And that feeling is a religious one. Its name is—faith.

What Sakharov cares for has very little connection with this basic religious problem in which the freedom of man and society is rooted. True, at the present time, signs of technocratic convergence are becoming more and more visible. If this is the basic path in the development of both systems, I will have to say, contrary to the people acclaiming convergence: "Unfortunately, convergence."

However, alongside Sakharov there exists Solzhenitsyn, and more and more often shoots of religious renaissance are appearing in Russia, although for the time being they are less noticeable than the public statements of scientists. But then the way to organic rather than mechanical convergence goes not through scientific-technical revolution, but through spiritual revolution, religious rebirth.

In a word: although the appearance of Sakharov and other Soviet scientists with demands for democratic liberties is a very gratifying phenomenon, the argument which they make and their platform of ideas do not stand up to criticism. Freedom is the goal. It cannot become a means for anything; scientific-technical convergence can have a positive meaning insofar as it serves individual and social freedom. Not vice versa.

Novi Sad, Yugoslavia, 1971

The Artist as the Enemy

To pose the question of why a man who creates novels, songs, poems, music, or paintings is considered the potential enemy of the social system under which he lives seems strange to me. No one who lives in a totalitarian society such as, say, the Chinese or the Soviet, would ask the question. It is clear without any explanation.

Is it possible that there are those who do not understand why a campaign was launched against Pasternak and his novel, *Doctor Zhivago*? Does anyone still wonder why Zhivago has not yet been published in Soviet Russia? How about Aleksandr Solzhenitsyn? It is a miracle that Solzhenitsyn is even alive. And free! One only needs to recall the martyrs of Russian literature of the last half-century; the names of those hundreds and hundreds killed or sent to forced-labor camps—Russian writers, painters, even musicians—to see why it is easy to be indignant when someone still asks why!

I will try to explain something which seems self-explanatory.

The great majority of artists who lost their lives in prison camps or those who are still there, like Andrei Sinyavsky, have never been political opponents of the regime in the Western sense. They were devoted to art. They minded their own business. They wrote, composed music, painted. Yet the powerful propaganda machine of those in authority tried to picture them as agents of imperialism, as dangerous enemies.

Looked at from the standpoint of maintaining a totalitarian dictatorship, the persecution of artists is wholly justified. One true artist is more dangerous to a totalitarian regime than any political adversary.

I repeat: Pasternak, Sinyavsky, Solzhenitsyn—they really

endanger and imperil the dictatorship of the Soviet Communist Party.

In order to explain the irreconcilable controversy between authentic art and Communist totalitarianism I will express in a few words the basic spiritual idea on which it is based. The essence is this: the world we live in is very bad. Everywhere there is disease, suffering, and injustice. This indicates that there is no reasonable Power above mankind (in case there is one it could only be an evil God, against whom it would be necessary to fight). There is only nature, which is hostile toward man. It is possible to create a paradise on earth. But to control nature one must submit to reason and discipline unorganized and imprudent human society. Society is like nature—that is, evil.

Society must first be organized on a reasonable, scientific basis. Such a society can be created only by a group of people, a Party. To be successful the Party must have absolute authority. Thus, power over nature is not possible without totalitarian dictatorship over people. And dictatorship is not possible without power to suppress human souls. The essence of all is *power*.

What has not been done to tame that most insubordinate reality, the human soul! First, it is demonstrated by erudite tracts that there are no souls—that the more man is subjugated the more free he is, etc., etc. This scholarly wisdom is backed up by crude police methods.

Sometimes, for years, this argument seems to have succeeded but then an imprisoned human soul comes flying into freedom, liberating other souls, smashing the spiritual basis of totalitarian authority.

At the beginning of the century the forerunner of socialist realism, Maxim Gorky, was convinced that, after the Revolution, in a "reasonably organized" Russia there would be at least a hundred writers of genius like Tolstoy. We know how such "organization" of Russia ended. We know of the thousands and thousands of totally untalented Soviet "writers" and "artists" who with their products created on the basis of party directives flood periodicals, exhibitions, concert halls, and film theaters in their country.

But art cannot be curbed. Power over human souls may be achieved only by lies. Art is a direct challenge to lies and hostile to the system on which power is based. This is why not only the novels of Solzhenitsyn but the music of Prokofiev was attacked in the USSR as inimical.

In a way our whole modern era is the enemy of art. We may be made prisoners not only by a one-party system but by a modern technological society whose only aim is material prosperity. The means of control of human souls are different there than in Communist countries, where power is more open and crude.

The collision of art with a social system is always a collision of freedom against repression, a combat of truth and lies, the struggle of life against deadening mechanism, and to put it into the language of religion—a fight between God and the Devil.

Novi Sad, Yugoslavia, 1970

The Way into the Impasse

There is an opinion, extraordinarily widespread, especially in the West, that the growth of national movements in totalitarian countries is only the first stage on the way to democratization and final recovery of the society from the cancerous tumor of totalitarianism.

At first glance that's the way it is. Examples tell us about it: Poland and Hungary in 1956; Czechoslovakia in 1968. Doubtless, the national Communist parties, leading the fight for their independence, immediately receive support from all national democratic forces. In a word, this way the unity of the totalitarian camp is destroyed and the citizens of the countries where so-called national communism has won receive somewhat more in the way of rights and liberties. Consequently, the growth of national movements in totalitarian countries, and especially in the USSR, is only to be acclaimed.

This is exactly the opinion which I regard as deeply mistaken and false. To see in the rebirth of nationalism a power resisting totalitarianism means not to apprehend the roots of the violently flourishing totalitarian dictatorships in our century.

Of course, the fight for national independence, like every other struggle for freedom, evokes sympathy and often exultation. However, I would venture to express a thought which will perhaps seem "heretical" to all enemies of totalitarianism: Internationalism was, is, and will be the greatest ideological power of communism; and until the idea of totalitarian internationalism is resisted by the idea of *antitotalitarian* internationalism, and the Communist pseudoreligion is supplanted by a true religion the presently dominant totalitarianism will be invincible. National movements will not subvert its foundations, but will only alter its form. "In order to conquer the lie of communism one has to admit its truth," the Russian philosopher Vladimir Solovyev wrote almost a century ago. And the truth of communism lies not only in its demands for social-economic justice, but also in its internationalism. Of course, one could point out that in reality there was never any internationalism in the Communist countries at all; however, that objection is not to the point because it does not touch on the very idea of "proletarian internationalism."

The breakup into national Communist movements does not signal the recovery of totalitarian countries, but only the furthest stage of the illness. National communism can be incomparably more intolerant toward democracy, stronger and more terrible; and the flirtation with democracy in the process of the struggle for independence from a single center is rapidly brought to nothing. Here is a big question: Where can one more easily conceive the future recovery of society, in dependent or independent totalitarian countries? It would not be bad to remind all those who have optimistic expectations for national rebirth about the existence of people who have been completely independent nationally and at the same time fervently totalitarian, like the German people during Hitler, the Italian people at the time of Mussolini, etc. And China, too, is presently independent.

Analyzing the aspirations of national forces at the critical moments in the struggle of the independence of "their" Communist parties—in Poland, Hungary, Czechoslovakia—we find demand everywhere for classical democratic liberties: freedom of speech, press, religion, political organizations, and strikes. Nothing in all these demands is exceptionally national—Polish, Hungarian, or Czech; and the demand for national independence of each of these countries is put forward as a necessary *condition* for the realization of the aforementioned democratic liberties. The expected liberties and democratic rights for which the struggle is being waged are not national, but *international*. And herein lies the basic tragedy and contradiction of all national movements. A truly democratic movement in totalitarian countries, dependent or independent, can only be international.

The truth of internationalism is that there exists spiritual realities far more important and deeper than national realities. The lie is that those realities are only of a class nature. Disintegration of the international Communist movements shows that Communist internationalism was built not on basic but on secondary realities. The recent renaissance of nationalism in the Communist world is in essence a step back, to *the initial positions.* The problems which gave rise to the powerful totalitarian movements of our century will remain unsolved for the future, until the appearance of an ideological force which will open the way to a true and not false internationalism; so-called "proletarian internationalism" will be invincible, even if all totalitarian countries become independent of any single center.

People are bound together not by the chance of nature or their origins, but by the community of undertaken tasks and strivings. I am convinced that one could have observed the very making of a *Communist nation,* the formation of even physical facial lines of party members, independent of their nationalities. Although this process is far from over yet, it was very much undermined by the Twentieth Congress of the Communist Party of the Soviet Union. In contrast to the French thinker Teilhard de Chardin, who felt that humanity can be divided into men who believe in progress and those who do not, I believe that the deepest division can be observed between people who believe in power and people who believe in freedom; people who believe in dictatorship, and people who believe in democracy, law, and order. The former are atheists, and the latter are religious people, whether they are aware of it or not, and no matter what they consider themselves to be.

Communists are men who believe in power and who are striving toward one thing—absolute power; however they may color themselves by nationality, they will not become democrats for that. Nor is belief in dictatorship or the striving toward power a national characteristic. The difference between those who believe in power and those who believe in freedom are considerably greater than any national characteristics. It seems to me that it will soon be apparent how totalitarian parties urge the national movements of "their" countries to clash with one another, in order to suppress the possibilities of international unification of the democratic forces of all totalitarian countries. And until there exists a more powerful idea of *true internationalism*, resulting exclusively from a religious rebirth, totalitarianism cannot be conquered by any national renaissance.

1971

The Shoots of Hope

What to do? How to live? In what to believe? Is there the slightest hope in our confused time for a real answer to these questions?

Every day millions of men ask themselves these questions and try in vain to answer them, observing closely the events of passing days. And these events, from all parts of the planet are flowing together and flashing, gleaming and disappearing on the television screen, as if through the window of an express train. With us, the passengers, remains only a grave impression that the world's absurdity is so great that there is no hope of finding sense in our life and no hope of a victory over chaos.

And indeed, where are the powers of resistance to the spiritual decay of all mankind? In the Eastern world, although the greatest of tyrants was dethroned fifteen years ago, recovery has nevertheless progressed little; so little that it does not seem strange at all that such a prominent Russian writer as Andrei Sinyavsky has since spent six years in a concentration camp; that Solzhenitsyn was undoubtedly saved from the same fate only by the Nobel Prize; that dozens of other Russian men, young and old, talented and not talented, paid for their independent views by a more terrible punishment—they found themselves in "psycho prisons"; that is, they were confined for an indefinite time in a madhouse. The Nazi doctor Mengele has not yet been caught, and a new one, a Soviet, Doctor Lunts, has already appeared, no less frightening. Of course, science and medicine have nothing to do with it, but it is also evident that no science alone can give or does give hope.

And in the West? Don't "gauchists" and "the New Left" reduce to zero every hope that the recovery of the world is possible? The Polish philosopher Laszek Kolakowski is completely right in regarding "the New Left"—all those "Mao-Tse-tung-ing" youth who believe in salvation by violence and dictatorship—as a symptom of the illness and not the cure. A symptom of that sinister illness which fifty years ago first struck Russia.

Do forces exist in the West which can resist the illness itself and not just its symptoms? I don't see them at the present time.

The main strength of all totalitarian movements of our century was, and is, the thirst for faith, the desperate wish to leave the solitary cell of one's soul at any price. What in the West can resist this craving toward totalitarianism? Science? It has nothing to do with it. The high standard of living? Not likely. Political democracy? But democracy itself needs a religious basis (although this often is not realized), and without it easily disintegrates.

And in Asia, each day the most fanatical and populous totalitarian power that the world has ever seen grows stronger and stronger; and one unwillingly remembers the prophecies of Nostradamus about the enslavement of Europe by the yellow race.

Above this turmoil of ideologies, parties, sects, leaders, and wars, the fear soars—as if forced on purpose by someone—that the planet may be destroyed by a world nuclear war. Fear is a bad ally, and it seems to me that it helps only the powers of organized chaos. Yet none of us now living on earth will be among the living in a hundred and fifty years at most, even if no war (or car accident for that matter) occurs. And that is why the fear of nuclear destruction is a false, invented fear binding the already enslaved powers of the human spirit.

But nevertheless, somewhere in the depths of his soul, man intuitively feels that both he and mankind are indestructible. Since it is impossible to eradicate this feeling, the powers of organized chaos and death try to drown it by external noise: slogans, shouts, marches, publicity. For a free man is deadly dangerous to the powers of organized chaos, and a man is free only when he feels that, somewhere in the depths of his soul, at the very center of centers called the "I," is something indestructible by any external power, be it laws of nature, violence or death. And the loss of this center is the most terrible thing that can happen to a man. And somewhere there, deep inside, the "I" of each of us is in contact with other "I's," and this very contiguity is love or religion. When the way to his own depth is closed in a man, then the unbearable solitude can be illusively overcome only in the superficial union with other human beings, who, like him, are alienated from their depths— namely, by joining such pseudoreligious movements as fascism, nazism, and communism. This is the whole essence of totalitarian movements. And no so-called highly developed scientific-industrial society can resist totalitarianism, because such a society, by its very structure, prepares the ground for totalitarian movements by enslaving man with an external rational-mechanical and technological structure of life. This, in turn, cuts off his way into his own depth, where true and not false unity (be it racial, class, or national) of human souls is rooted and where there is always cosmos and never chaos. A lack of belief in a suprapersonal and real tie of our deep personalities separates us. Only when through the depth of one's "I" one feels the reality of other "I's" is political democracy possible and vice versa: When man is cut off from his deep roots he does not feel the reality of somebody else's "I," and he easily inclines violence toward others.

But this is most interesting: while depressingly large numbers of young people in the West are leaning toward totalitarianism, their counterparts in the already formed totalitarian systems are emerging with exactly contrary demands, demands for all that the Western youth regard as "passe," "bourgeois prejudices": freedom of speech, freedom of the press, legality. And how can one evaluate the more and more frequent appearances in Russia of a new, reborn religiosity among young people who have lived all their lives in a particularly atheistic society? One remembers the words of Guiseppe Mazzini: "In the sufferings of slavery people are learning to love freedom."

And if it is true that the lights from solitude into totalitarian movements ends in slavery (and the whole history of the twentieth century attests to that), then the horrible sufferings of slavery by some emotional processes unknown to us are opening to man a way into the depths of his soul, thus liberating him from the solitude that pushed him towards totalitarianism. In this way a foundation is created for a free, democratic, organic, and not totalitarian-mechanical society—this time not of national but of planetary dimensions.

A comparison unavoidably arises between present-day Russia, the country with the longest lasting totalitarianism, and the situation of Raskolnikov, hero of Dostoyevsky's novel *Crime and Punishment*, during his sojourn in the hard-labor camp. It seems that the day of a miracle approaches, that moment when the murderer, after having suffered his sin of violence, is again able to love; that is, to live. The youth of the West, unfortunately, are too much like Raskolnikov at the time when he was just prepared to commit violence.

The latest books of underground Soviet literature startled one with the deep comprehension of what is happening in the world. At the same time that the United Nations agency UNESCO was celebrating the jubilee of the "great humanist" Lenin, the posthumous novel-confession *All Flows* of Vasily Grossman, once a well-known "social realist," revealed with great power the image of Lenin as the creator of the most slavish of all social systems existing in history. In the West the intelligentsia is becoming more and more "Left," and conservatives-traditionalists consider it possible to fight against totalitarianism with military-technical and economic advantages. Yet at the same time Nadezhda Mandelstam, the wife of the prominent poet who perished in the labor camps, writes that just as Russia once saved Europe from the invasion of Tartars, now Russia will save Western civilization from rationalism, which engenders that loneliness from which totalitarianism stems. She thinks that Russia can and must find strength in itself to triumph over totalitarianism, because totalitarianism is invincible from the outside.

No political movement, no carefully elaborated social system, no science or technology, can bring sense to our world and conquer chaos at the present time. It can be achieved only by the true religious renaissance suffered through in one's own experience. It appears necessary to travel to the end of the road of oppression and evil actively believing in it, or passively submitting to it, in order to cease forever to believe in the power and invincibility of evil. And paradoxically, it can be said that without these endlessly long years of totalitarian dictatorship, tomorrow's freedom could not appear in Russia. And this freedom will of course have nothing in common with totalitarianism.

The biggest question is whether it is possible to come to that true freedom, democratic legality, organic order, without going through the illness of totalitarianism. On the answer to that question depends the fate of the West. Maybe the threat of Asiatic totalitarianism will speed up the course of the illness and the recovery? But where are the shoots of hope in the West? The students, the poor, the colored population, all those in whom Marcuse believes, are more or less infected by the spirit of violence, which means the totalitarian spirit.

In the prophetic novel by George Orwell, *1984*, which depicts the whole world in the grips of three totalitarian superstates, the hero feels that the only hope for mankind is the "proles," proletariat not infected by the spirit of a totalitarian party. And now, in the turmoil of the world's absurdity, which in many ways confirms the vision of Orwell's genius, one can rightfully say that the only hope is in those "Zeks," that is, the prisoners of Soviet labor camps, whose lives and thoughts are the living hope, giving sense to our lives, too. And our sufferings, hourly aroused by tormenting questions and the absurdity of television emissions, are becoming more tolerable because, as Nietzsche said, it is not that man can't endure great sufferings but that senseless sufferings are unbearable.

So, those shoots of hope, appearing where they were least expected, presently provide the only answer to the questions posed at the beginning of this article.

Belgrade, Yugoslavia, 1971

Three Paradoxes

The birth of planetary consciousness is not yet recognized. In what can one see characteristics of this emerging consciousness? Are some elements which are to be its component parts already apparent? It seems to me that it is already possible to clearly observe *three paradoxical phenomena* inherent in the planetization of mankind.

At one time a hero of one of Dostoyevsky's novels posed this moral-theological question: What would you choose, if it was proposed that you could become rich and happy if you would allow in return that one man would lose his life in faraway China, or on the moon, without anybody but you ever knowing? In our time such a question ceases to be theoretical and becomes particularly practical. And this is what is *paradoxical:* right now, in the flood of social immorality of every kind, moral laws which once appeared to people as abstract, have become physical laws available for observation and research. It is impossible to suppress freedom on the other side of the planet and at the same time not suppress it at home. It is impossible to do violence to anyone else, and at the same time not experience it oneself. Evil is international and planetary, and the increase of evil on one part of the planet can be felt everywhere.

Whatever we wish, there are no longer any isolated phenomena and events in the world. All, everything that is happening, has a direct relation to every one of us. This process of all-dependence and all-penetration the French philosopher Teilhard de Chardin called "the formation of noosphere"— the only spiritual organism of all mankind. And although it sometimes seems to us that in relation to the immensity of totalitarian mechanisms man alone is completely powerless, it is *paradoxical* that this very totalization of the world can infinitely intensify and add universal meaning to every vital impulse toward the freedom of one person. Where else can only one word, article, speech, book, even silence shake society to its foundations and have such meaning and power as in the USSR, for instance?

Totalization of the world has reached such dimensions that there is no one phenomenon—not just in politics, but also in the religious sphere, in science, in art, in philosophy—which would not provoke a sharp response, positive or negative, in every man presently living on earth.

And here is the third *paradox:* with the growth of specialization in all fields of human activity—art, technology, knowledge, in all professions—*specialized questions are disappearing;* every stir of thought becomes something on which the life and destiny of each of us depends.

This phenomenon is especially apparent in the development of scientific thought. Here is, for instance, something which might previously have provoked only the interest of specialists: the apparatus used by Professor Delgado of Yale University for the control of brain reactions and the flow of emotions. Now the world is becoming familiar with the horrific possibilities of such activities known already by those acquainted with the all-embracing power, uncontrollability, and amorality of totalitarian societies. That which the whole cultural world would previously have regarded only as a regional demonstration of primordial barbarism—namely the Soviet Union's imprisonment in madhouses of mentally healthy people for their political beliefs—is now as a result of the totalization of the world a realistic horror menacing every man daily. It is not by chance that in Russia the Hippocratic oath which doctors throughout the world have taken for centuries, was changed this year into a new, Soviet one, obliging doctors to serve not only a sick man but also "Communist society," "party and the people." Is it possible to overestimate the planetary importance of such an ominous phenomenon?

Or take, for instance, the conviction still held among wide segments of the world population that the world is divided into the poor and the rich, and that such a division disappears with the abolition of private property. Those holding this conviction fail completely to discern the form and the content of power and fail to comprehend the fact that power doesn't need private property at all, and that the political monopoly in the USSR or China bestows an absolute power to the party magnates beyond the dreams of capitalists. Yesterday one could regard all this as only the normal unenlightenment of the masses and their characteristic lack of thought, but today it is a threatening and sinister ground for the demagogues of the ardent dictatorship.

In my opinion, the following three paradoxical phenomena in the spiritual life of mankind will become component parts of the future planetary consciousness:

1. Moral laws, which before seemed abstract and in need of ideological, legal, or religious substantiation, are now becoming physically tangible.

2. Totalization of the world infinitely intensifies the action of one person, augmenting the threat of such an action to the extent of the loss of life.

3. Universal and all-embracing specialization eliminates all specialized questions.

In spite of the development of science, the widening of horizons in all the fields of knowledge, etc., etc., the future planetary consciousness is returning to the most elementary existential questions, facing man now just as they did ten-thousand years ago. Upon the answers to those questions depends the solution of all the other questions, political, scientific, and philosophical. Science, philosophy, politics, and social order are not solving the existential problem of man, but vice versa; science, philosophy, and social order depend on their solution. And existential questions are being solved by every man separately. All this leads to the basic problem, which is the religious problem, that is, the problem of the relation of the individual toward life, toward death, toward the universe.

In relation to the planetary consciousness, all current ideologies—those of nation, class, race, and so on—are simply provincial.

Belgrade, 1971

Religious Rebirth

Planetary consciousness, the birth of which can soon be expected, leads to the existential questions, which, in their turn, are decided by each man separately, depending on his feeling of the link between his own existence and the whole life of the planet, the life of the universe—which means depending on his religion. Because religion is the very *link*.

In the last century Dostoyevsky sought to prove that there is only one idea without which human life is impossible, and that is the idea of the immortality of the individual soul. In our century Teilhard de Chardin took the same view, but in relation to the whole of mankind: it is impossible to believe in progress and the future of mankind without belief in the immortality of mankind.

Today, when there are no more questions which are exclusively political, religious, medical, chemical, etc., the idea of immortality of the human soul assumes not only a universal but a practical political meaning. Never before has the question of personal immortality been posed so sharply to each man— not theoretically but in fact—as in the present totalitarian societies. If physical death is the end, then slavery is justified. Then; it is indeed better to be a living slave carrying out unquestioningly the directions of the party than not to be at all. And vice versa—if the soul, the "I" of each of us, is immortal, then worship of outside violence is the loss of the soul, which is worse than the loss of life. Thus in totalitarian societies one can observe the rebirth of the religious life's purpose, which the nineteenth century seemed to have completely rejected.

It is extraordinarily instructive to read Soviet underground and semiunderground literature such as Pasternak's novel, *Doctor Zhivago*, works by Solzhenitsyn, the novel-confession

All Flows by Grossman, *Reminiscences* by Nadezhda Mandelstam. In all these works one feels the awareness that the prison of totalitarianism was not undeserved. The longer the punishment lasts, the more clear it becomes that man was of course guilty, not politically, but metaphysically. Analyzing Stalin's purges one unavoidably concludes that the Biblical proverb, "Those who live by the sword shall die by the sword," was empirically proved in the history of the Russian revolution. The more one reads the memoirs of Soviet prisoners the more one becomes permeated with the paradoxical conviction that there was *no injustice* done, but that a mystical justice was manifesting itself all the time. The worst punished were men who most believed in communism; that is, in the compulsory reorganization of the world.

On the other hand, who can forget, in Solzhenitsyn's story "One Day in the Life of Ivan Denisovich," the character of Alyosha the Baptist, who, even in the horror of the labor camp was living a full emotional life, and about whom the author himself wrote that "prison is to him like water off a duck's back." So, the paradoxical consciousness—inherent only in the people who went through the hell and purgatory of totalitarianism—that in the world there is no real justice leads toward consciousness of one's own responsibility for one's own and the world's destiny. Society is not guilty, the world is not bad, but man himself is guilty, although his sin almost always lies in the obedience to external violence, or the active faith in violence. Thus simultaneously with the psychology of personal guilt a free man is born.

The religious, philosophical question about whether there is justice in the universe becomes in our time a practical question; and on its answer depends everything—our life, history, and the future of mankind. Since this question is most acute in Russia, the religious rebirth can be expected to come from there. The Soviet Union, like the Roman Empire, has prepared the soil for the planetary religious rebirth.

Religious rebirth is not a theoretical or ideological matter. There is no need for an all-embracing theory giving precepts of what to do. Rather, one has to be able again to feel in oneself that internal compass which every minute of life shows the only right direction for action, to have faith in it, and to follow its directions, despite any deadly threats.

About this, Pasternak wrote in *Doctor Zhivago:* "The whole tragedy started from the fact that we ceased to believe our own opinion."

To live trusting our inward feelings means to live a religious life. But what punishments and purges are still awaiting us in order that we might be capable of so living? Even in his time, Plato thought that "the ancients were better than we are and were living closer to the gods." And it seems to our epoch that Plato himself lived in an enchanted epoch of closeness to gods.

Belgrade, 1971

Russia And Communism

This article is not an historical survey, but simply an attempt to analyze the odd fact that such a great number of ex-Communists, after being disillusioned with the Communist utopia, turn their hatred against not the Communist myth, but instead national and historical Russia. And it happens precisely with the ex-Communists!

Vasily Grossman in his novel *Forever Flowing*, which was much talked about, and deservedly so, for its radical criticism of Lenin, bluntly claims that in Russia, as opposed to the West, social progress has always been accompanied by a reinforcement of slavery. He wrote: "Development of the West was engendered by the growth of freedom, and the development of Russia by the growth of slavery. . . . Russian progress and Russian slavery were bound together by a thousand-year-old chain. After the October Revolution Russian slavery will have crossed Russian borders and become a torch lighting new ways for humanity. . . . Lenin's synthesis of nonfreedom and socialism stunned the world to a greater degree than the discovery of atomic energy. . . . The thousand-year-old Russian law of development became a universal law. . . ."[1]

The East German party heretic Wolfgang Garich says that "the forms that socialism acquired in the Soviet Union are historically conditioned quite apart from Russian backwardness and the lack of democratic traditions. . . ."[2] He is echoed by Arkadii Belinkov in his article "The Land of Slaves, the Land of Masters," which is full of hatred for Russia: "In that land, which never learned what freedom is, and which never needed freedom . . . the main task of Russian history has always been to try to stifle freedom. And . . . the Russian intelligentsia was always ready to help in that endeavor. . . . In such a country as Russia, where the educated circles and the common people are corrupted and depraved by the hereditary slavery and slave-owning, fear, national tradition and historical tradition, freedom was never needed. . . ."[3]

Even Milovan Djilas, the most important of ex-Communists, in his book *Conversations with Stalin*, tends to shove the sins of Stalinism onto the shoulders of "historical Russian imperialism and chauvinism." Almost the only exception to this line of thinking are the statements of the Polish philosopher Laszek Kolakowski: "The worst service that can be rendered to the cause of Polish independence and democracy is the strengthening in the society of traditional, nationalistic anti-Russian clichés. The Russian people, who were put through the most terrible Gehenna in contemporary history, are still being used as an instrument of imperialistic policy by its rulers. But Russia is itself a victim of that policy, more than any other nation. Those people who, instead of developing knowledge and understanding of the genuine Russian national culture are satisfied with the strengthening of anti-Russian clichés, are unwittingly helping the power which has enslaved both nations."[4]

This tendency to cast slurs upon the historical Russia is not only noticeable among Russian ex-Communists, but it is also spreading in the Communist countries which are independent of the Soviet Union. In China the clichés are repeated endlessly about the imperialist policies of "Moscow tsars" which allegedly have been continued by the Soviet leadership in betraying the ideals of communism. In Yugoslavia, where Grossman's *Forever Flowing* was published last year, and not banned, there is still no hope whatsoever that the books of Nadezhda Mandelstam, revealing the spiritual basis of every kind of communism, will ever be published.

It is very interesting to note that all those people who blame historical Russia for the sins of the Communist dictatorship, no matter how different their present ideological and political positions are, have one thing in common: their atheism. They are all atheists, just like Marx, who also hated Russia fiercely.

So where in essence are the roots of the Communist dictatorship's half-century of obscurantism? Are they in the purely Western theory of Marxism and the "dictatorship of the proletariat" on the road to the "kingdom of freedom"; or are they in the "half-Asiatic" imperialistic religious tradition of Russia? What is national Russia: hangman or victim?

On the answer to that question depends so very, very much. Like, for example, the ability of Western European Communists to persuade us that in their respective European countries communism will have quite a different face from that in "Asiatic Russia." Certainly there is no proof of that assurance, as yet. All the "non-Soviet" communisms differ little from the Soviet one, and they are mainly outside of Europe, in countries like Cuba, or China. One cannot take as examples such European countries as Albania—which is independent of the Kremlin—or the semidependent Romania. In those two countries, in some respects, the Communist dictatorship has outdone even the Soviet one. There remains only Yugoslavia, but here, for the time being, "the avant-garde of the working class" has evidently relinquished its leadership in such spheres as industry (Yugoslavia has a free market) and culture (there is no social realism). However, venomous tongues say that it was precisely that *deviation* from Marxism-Leninism (in any case from Leninism) and the absence of party monopoly in leadership in these spheres that made Yugoslavia the freest and richest country in the Communist camp. But judging by current events, that situation can be easily cured.

One thing is clear: if the "failure" to build the Communist society occurred because of historical characteristics and the backwardness of Russia, then Marx was basically right. The struggle to establish the "dictatorship of the proletariat" in the

Western and non-Western countries makes sense and could go on, and the faith in the "kingdom of freedom," despite the Soviet Union, would remain unshaken. That is approximately what the various "Left" and "New Left" people think.

However, it might be the case that in the beginning of the century, before the February Revolution and before the Bolsheviks usurped power in October 1917, Russia was not such a backward Asiatic country. This is the way it was described by the English historian Tibor Samueli:

> The most autocratic tsars were gentle and benevolent rulers compared with their Communist successors. There are very few people abroad who know the degree of freedom of tsarist Russia at the beginning of our century. The censorship was abolished and there was a completely free press. Even the Bolshevik publications were published without limitations. There was also in Russia a complete freedom to travel abroad, there existed independent trade unions, an independent court, jury and a progressive system of social legislation. There was a Parliament, called the Duma, which consisted of representatives of parties of all shades of opinion, including the Bolsheviks. Nowadays we can regard the pre-Revolutionary Russia as a model of democracy, and compared with the 126 countries—members of the United Nations—it would come out as one of 15 or 20 of the most liberal countries in the world.[5]

If this is true, then of course Marxism and Leninism are to blame for the existence of such an inhumane social order as the Soviet one. It is then not the fault of the historical tradition of Russia; it is the struggle of the Communist Party for power in the whole world which would lead mankind straight into the totalitarian hell.

The picture of Russian life in the last century, as depicted by classical Russian literature, as compared with the spirit of the orthodox Soviet literature is sufficient to understand whether the root of slavery is in historical Russia or in European Marxism. Marx, in his idea of "dictatorship of the proletariat," had already attained the synthesis of socialism and slavery. Lenin only perfected the idea in practice, with the characteristic Russian depth of faith, but a faith in the idea of Marx.

The only question we can ask is why communism won its first victory in Russia. Was it because of Moscow's traditional messianic aspirations to be the Third Rome and the inborn religiosity of the Russian people? There is no doubt that the messianic side of communism (which acquired an extremely imperialistic character in the "dictatorship of the proletariat") is very dear to the Russian soul. But messianism per se is in no way connected with the *forceful* organization of an "earthly paradise."

If one does not regard the religious intensity of the Russian people as a backwardness and shortcoming (as almost every disillusioned Communist does) one has to admit that this very powerful religiosity helped to *expose* so early and so ultimately the wickedness of *the faith* in a Communist Utopia. Certainly in a less religious nation, the true spirit of Marxism would not have manifested itself so quickly. But that fact would not have made Marxism any less immoral. To blame the Russian people and not Marxism for the intensity of faith in the Marxist ideology is absolutely nonsensical.

I believe that the reason for the anti-Russian feelings of ex-Communists (let alone those of the active non-Russian Communists) is hidden in their yet persistent faith in a Communist Utopia.

Therefore, the atheism. Because essentially there are only two faiths in the world: the belief in God, the Creator of life and the universe, who made our souls immortal and consequently free; and the faith in the possibility of organizing an earthly paradise by human effort and understanding. That latter faith means to achieve earthly paradise by coercion, which is of course impossible if there is a God and he created the human soul immortal and free.

Thus, the inevitable premise of the struggle against any Communist and non-Communist totalitarianism is the criticism of atheism

1973

NOTES

1. Vasily Grossman; *Forever Flowing*, trans. Thomas P. Whitney (N.Y.: Harper Row), 1972. The quotation was translated by the author from the Russian edition published by Possev, 1970, pp. 178-81.

2. *Bitter Harvest*, Praeger, New York, 1961, p. 325.

3. *The New Bell*, London, 1972, pp. 348, 355, 358.

4. *Culture*, (Polish-Russian periodical), no. 2, pp. 56-57.

5. Afterword by T. Samueli to the book *Half Marx* by Tufton Beamish, London, 1970.

The Phenomenology of the Kingdom of Lies

The book entitled *Stalinism as a Spiritual Phenomenon* by Roman Redlikh, which appeared last year in the edition of the Possev publishing house, is in my opinion itself a spiritual phenomenon of paramount importance. The absence of broad response and numerous commentaries, which were expected not only in the Russian free press but also in other free presses, is puzzling to me and can hardly be explained by the mere fact that the book had one or even two previous printings (if one counts the editions on rotary press in the years 1949-52).

As it happens, only now, after having read writings by Solzhenitsyn, Sinyavsky, Grossman, Nadezhda Mandelstam, Amalrik, and Pomerantz, can one fathom the depths of this remarkable analysis of the spiritual foundations and the complicated mechanisms of Soviet society. What is startling is the fact that the book, which is literally a scientific-theoretical commentary on the works of the aforementioned Russian authors, was written long before the appearance of those works. Those works empirically confirm the methodological premises of the author of *Stalinism as a Spiritual Phenomenon*.

In the West, many people will certainly not understand or will not want to understand this book. The reason for that is the same as the reason why in the Soviet Union, as Mr. Redlikh shows with a genuine spiritual clairvoyance, many people prefer not to learn the whole truth about the nature of the Communist power—not from fear of "agents," but from fear of the consequences this knowledge would lead to. Nevertheless, the potential readers of the book *Stalinism as a Spiritual Phenomenon* are in the East, and I do not doubt at all that the East is where the book will in the future be completely appraised and understood. I don't know of any better and more serious theoretical book about Soviet society, and generally about communism in all its forms; and I am deeply convinced that it will in time become an indispensable textbook for anyone who wants to understand everything that happens—what, how, and why—wherever the Communist Party holds the monopoly of power.

The Russian religious philosopher Berdyaev earlier wrote in his article "Spirits of the Russian Revolution" that "they [the Bolsheviks] are dealing with fictions and not realities; and they are changing the entire economic life of Russia into fiction." Now then, the most precious, original, and fundamental idea of Redlikh is more than just his demonstration that the indispensable methodological premise of any study of Soviet society is the ability to differentiate between the world of Soviet reality and its official description by the Communists. He also shows that *the analysis of the relations* between the reality and the official fictions gives us *the key to understanding* the mechanisms of the Communist Party of the Soviet Union in all the spheres of Soviet spiritual life. The analysis of that power mechanism and its attitude toward the values it serves forms the basic content of the book. The new terminology which Redlikh introduces into the study of Soviet society, such as "active nonfreedom," "fictionalism," "exoteric and esoteric content of communism," "consciousness," etc. will become indispensable to every serious sociological study of totalitarian societies of the Communist type.

The claim that communism is a pseudo-religion is not novel, nor is the realization that the idea of the "kingdom of freedom and justice" is only a means to reinforce the Communist monopoly. (In the words of Orwell in his novel *1984*, "the dictatorship is not introduced to protect the revolution, but the revolutions are performed in order to introduce the dictatorship.") What is new in Redlikh's book is his demonstration that, (1) the inner, esoteric content of communism *cannot be theoretically expressed*, since it is the *will toward power per se* (which was not realized by the first generation of Bolsheviks) and consequently it cannot survive without myths and fictions; and (2) those very myths and fictions themselves become instruments of power even when the subjects cease to believe in them.

The will for totalitarian power over the world always presupposes the exclusive existence of one visible world. Therefore, despite all the created myths about the future of communism and "the kingdom of freedom," communism does not become a religion but remains pseudo-religious, or as Berdyaev puts it, false religion. From this fact stems the necessary duality and lie of communism.

The will for absolute power, then, is the fundamental inner force of communism. But since it is impossible to have power over the spiritual world, communism makes every effort to destroy spiritual life, to replace it with a fictitious one over which it has power and which itself serves as the instrument of enslavement. Thus, for instance, all history is replaced by fictitious history. Real history cannot, of course, be abolished because man does not have power over that which has happened; but fictitious history serves perfectly the cause of spiritual enslavement. This way, in all the spheres of spiritual life, every force of Communist fictionalism is directed not toward making people think in a Communist way but toward making them *not think at all*. All the slave-owning societies in history have limited the freedom of men; but Soviet society is the first in history in which Redlikh's term "active nonfreedom" applies, because that society demands not only obedience from its subjects but an active participation in the lie and fictionalism. As Redlikh puts it, "active nonfreedom" is "that state in which the thoughts, desires, and feelings of a man cease to play any role whatsoever in his behavior."

The whole system of spiritual fictionalism leaves a vivid mark on the Russian language. "To accuse Stalinism of having cluttered and mutilated the Russian language," says Redlikh, "is like mourning the beautiful hair of a chopped-off head. Stalinism does not mutilate or clutter the language, it destroys it. . . . In the semantic structure of words created in the Bolshevik period or of words whose meanings were changed (which happens more often) there appears a completely new function which is absent in the non-Bolshevik words. We are going to call that function fictionalistic." The task of such a mortification of the language is the same as the task of positive and negative myths and fictions. It consists, in the words of Redlikh, of "bankrupting the concepts which represent positive ideals that contradict the idea of active nonfreedom and transforming such notions as freedom, happiness, humanism, democracy, into fictional notions. In that manner, the very possibility of calling things by their real names in the USSR is liquidated."

The chapter in the book dealing with the psychology of Soviet man, his duality, and "the secret layer of consciousness inside him" will assuredly give birth to a whole new field in psychology—the psychology of man in totalitarian society, a branch which has very little in common with the psychoanalysis of Freud, Adler, or Jung. The book's demonstration that the skepticism of Soviet man is vested religion and that his cynicism is vested conscience represents the author's remarkable insight. And although Redlikh writes that the total history of the Soviet period is the history of a struggle between the people and the party, he nevertheless realizes that bolshevism has something in common with the age-old Russian idea of "serving" the common cause, and that is exactly why the sickness of Communist totalitarianism in Russia is so tragic and so long-lasting.

Only his deep love for Russia and consequently his hatred

for communism has given the author spiritual vision and at the same time acute realism and scientific objectivity. It was Redlikh's objectivity that made him admit that the liberation from the sickness of totalitarianism cannot occur on the superficial political level, i.e., externally and socially. On the contrary it requires inner heroism and the conquest of the fear that exists in the soul of every Soviet man, a fear consciously planted there by the authorities. For all of us who believe in the future victory over the evil of totalitarian enslavement, the following words from the book *Stalinism as a Spiritual Phenomenon* should become an axiom:

> The secret layer of the soul of Soviet men is a reservoir of hidden powers, of an enormous tension. To set those powers free means to deal Stalinism a mortal blow. But those powers are in essence not destructive but constructive. This feature of the contemporary Russian soul has to be taken into account by every defender of freedom. To set those powers free also means to free the greatest creative possibilities and to create conditions for uncovering a new mental and spiritual structure of man's personality. The liberation from the yoke of the active nonfreedom is the liberation not of an old creature of a passing era but of a new man, who has been put through the spiritually tragic test of Stalinism and who has survived that most terrible trial.

The second volume of the book, which is in preparation, arouses great interest. It is supposed to analyze Soviet society after the death of Stalin, when "Stalinism" underwent some changes, but remained spiritually the same old kingdom of lies whose mechanisms were exposed so substantially and deeply by Redlikh.

Belgrade, 1972

On Responsibility: Marx and Lenin in Their Personal Lives

Several books have appeared lately revealing little-known facts about the personal lives of "scientific socialism's" two leading figures. From Valentinov's book *The Little Known Lenin*[1] the reader learns such awkward things as the fact that Lenin loved the good life, loved always to have money to spend, and enjoyed good food and the theater; even during World War I when meatless days were introduced in Switzerland, Lenin and Krupskaya (his wife) disregarded them and indulged themselves with meat "patties." Although he had unlimited faith in his own historical "mission," Lenin did not feel shy about taking money from his family and from "capitalist fools" sympathetic to the Revolution. To secure this money he tried often in his letters to appear very poor.

In the book *Karl Marx—a Psychogram*[2] the Swiss sociologist Arnold Küntzli describes in unsympathetic terms the personal and family life of Marx. The truth of the matter is that Marx's family with his many children spent almost all their lives in terrible poverty, even in destitution, all because Marx did not want to provide for them by normal work, even by tutoring languages. He believed only in his mission, and wrote his Marxist works while cadging money from Engels and pawning his wife's last things. As a result of all this his children were dying, his wife was tormented, and who knows how it all would have ended had not his well-to-do friend Engels at last granted a small yearly pension to the family. The moral side of Marx's life also left a lot to be desired. His concealment of an illegitimate child he had with a maid is of course not suitable as an example for young generations of Communists to follow.

Undoubtedly, these books are very useful (as is any truth), especially after countless hack biographies of the two "coryphaei," portraying Marx and Lenin as shining figures with only good qualities and virtues. However, I believe it is extremely important to stress that the unpleasant traits in the personal lives of these men speak as little against Marxism-Leninism as the hack stories of their lives speak for Marxism-Leninism.

A writer who, with poisonous satisfaction, tries to represent Marx and Lenin as irresponsible toward their families, to reproach Marx for living only for his "mission" and not supporting his family and for "stubbornly refusing to earn his daily bread even in the face of his children's deaths,"[3] employs the same set of values used by the hack Soviet biographers. Such cheap writing is based on worthless notions about human responsibility. The problem of responsibility is much more complicated and tragic than it appears to Soviet and anti-Soviet biographers. It requires a lot of hard thinking.

Even irreconcilable ideological enemies admit that "Lenin was absolutely alien to base motives, personal ambitions . . . he was incorruptible, unselfish [if one does not count the meat "patties"—M. M.], he worked indefatigably."[4] Marx also did not spare himself or his family and worked all his life in the harshest of circumstances, unwilling to use his brain power for some work that would materially take care of his family, although his pawning and sponging activities, in the words of his biographer Küntzli, "doubtless cost him far more in expenditure of time and nervous energy than, for example, teaching languages, as he could have done." [5] There is no doubt, therefore, that both Marx and Lenin were serving, in the fullest sense of the word, an idea that transcended themselves.

Let's put aside the question of what kind of idea that was and to what ends that idea led comtemporary mankind. Some even say that without Marx and Lenin the imminent spiritual revolution we are beginning to see now in the socialist world would have been impossible. Some authors, by no means Communist ones, maintain that Marx and Lenin responded to God's eternal call, "Who is going to carry my message?" and received a command to go and bedazzle mankind. I am reminded that it was the Russian religious philosopher Lev Shestov who wrote that it is very useful to "let matter go to heaven"[6] for a period of time; that was exactly the result of the endeavors of our two "coryphaei."

This is the main point: both Marx and Lenin were perfectly aware of their responsibility to serve their cause and they sacrificed for that service all they had, despite their materialistic theories.

In accusing Marx of not wanting to take care of his family first, instead of the idea he served, his critics evidently do not realize they are treading a slippery path where it is easy to stumble. Wasn't Dostoyevsky also pawning his wife's clothes? Did not Turgenev have illegitimate children with maids? Or take, for example, Gauguin—why did he have to leave his wife, his children, and a well-paying job in a Paris bank to hang about Tahiti, living in want with a native woman and only painting, painting, painting? How about the moral qualities of Pushkin? How many hundreds of his mistresses did his biographers come up with? And Richard Wagner—did he not unscrupulously take advantage of his rich admirers? How about Rimbaud, Esenin, Osip Mandelstam, Tchaikovsky? They certainly were not holding steady jobs and receiving paychecks every first day of the month. Were they not begging? *Almost all* men who ever contributed something new to art, science, culture, philosophy, even religion, were in genuinely tragic positions when they had to make a choice between serving that imperious inner call and "blind faith" (of which biographers accuse Marx and Lenin) and caring for their families, everyday earnings, public opinion, generally accepted moral standards, and other things along that line.

It has always been like that, and it is doubtful that it will ever change. Not just hacks write of this, but unfortunately critical biographers also. It evidently never occurred to either side, for example, that Marx's refusal to earn his living by such intellectual work as "tutoring languages," even when faced with the deaths of his children, whom he truly loved, was proof of that unearthly call which he followed "not knowing where he was going . . . " (to use Biblical words). Men who have never felt that inner call are of course outraged that some energetic, talented people (Marx was far from being lazy), instead of using their gifts to feed their families, prefer to struggle and expend incredible effort on the humiliating practice of begging because they do not want to use their talent for something that has nothing to do with their "mission."

It is strange that nobody even raises the question of why Marx preferred to earn his living not by teaching but by begging, which cost him much more effort and nervous energy (a fact that even his critical biographer, the pedantic Swiss Küntzli admits). Why is it that Spinoza did not give lessons in Latin and philosophy, but preferred to earn his living as a glass grinder?

The answer to that question could be very interesting indeed. Maybe it would be no different from the answer of a faithful wife, who could be asked why she prefers hard and dirty work, and sometimes even begging, when she could earn money much more easily by cheating sometimes on her beloved. Why, she is so beautiful and loves so beautifully!

The problem is not only that genius and generally accepted morality, or ordinary decency, are, as everyone knows, very rarely compatible. If one is to be guided by generally accepted moral consideration, one would have to repudiate even Pushkin, which the Russian religious philosopher Vladimir Solovyev did, in a perfectly consistent way. Naturally, in this case another difficulty arises, and that is: What about people such as Hitler or the notorious inquisitor Torquemada who in their personal lives and morals could serve as an example, because they did not indulge in debauchery, or perhaps did not drink, or did not smoke, or even eat meat?

No, the entire problem is much more complicated, and it pertains to the question of the responsibility of each of us ordinary men, and not only of a genius.

I think that in Liuben'kyi [the infamous prison in Moscow—trans.] the interrogator always poses the following question to prisoners who are members of a democratic movement or some other movement resisting the Communist dictatorship: "Young man, you have a wife and child, why do you have to ask for trouble? Think about them, think about the fate you are dooming them to."

So, there it is: responsibility juxtaposed to responsibility. Which one to choose? Responsibility toward your family or responsibility toward Russia, freedom, one's soul? Who would be brave enough to throw a stone at those people who deliberately commit themselves to martyrdom, and their families to beggary? Or who could reproach them for lack of responsibility? Where is the judge who knows for sure which responsibility is more important? Arnold Küntzli will hardly find in the Gospel the proof to support his accusation that Marx was irresponsible.

To conclude: both Marx and Lenin have in their theoretical, ideological, and political activity so much that merits the most vigorous criticism, censure, and condemnation (to begin with, naturally, their militant atheism) that to reproach them for eating meat patties and being unwilling to tutor languages, and to call them irresponsible for these very reasons, is, I maintain, to do something that could bring about the very antithesis of the desired results.

1973

NOTES

1. V. Valentinov: *The Little Known Lenin*, Paris, 1972.
2. Based on the article by Aglaya Austen "The Teacher of Life," *Russian Thought*, August 2, 1973.
3. Ibid.
4. B. Suvarin, "Introduction" to V. Valentinov's *The Little Known Lenin*.
5. Based on the article by Aglaya Austen, "The Teacher of Life."
6. Lev Shestov, *On the Scales of Job*, p. 149, Paris, 1928.

Letter to a Friend in the West

Dear Friend:

I have been slow in answering your letter not because the circumstances of my life are unfavorable for this kind of spiritual-ideological correspondence (although they are), or because it is difficult for me to raise objections to the thoughts expressed in your letters, which I of course do not agree with. No, that is not the case. I have started to answer you several times and put it off. I could not bring myself to do it. If you were my ideological enemy everything would be all right. The bewilderment would not torment me then, and it would be very easy to write. You are not my enemy, however, but my friend and that is why the problem arose before me as how to show you (not convince you but *show* you) something that is self-evident to me and that you cannot see. The main problem was: Why should I do it at all? For if your own life, the world you are living in, and all the books and newspapers you are reading, produce in you judgments which I regard as deeply mistaken, what importance could my answer have to you?

I am reminded of that young Italian Communist girl described in the autobiography of Eugenia Ginzburg, *Journey into the Whirlwind.* I don't know if you have read that book, but those in Italy especially should read it. . . . That Italian girl escaped before the Second World War from Fascist Italy to the "motherland of all workers," naturally got into Stalin's torture chambers, and was seen by the author somewhere in the prison's cellar at the moment they were water-hosing her in freezing weather. Obviously understanding nothing the girl was shouting, "Io sono Communista, Io sono Communista"—I am a Communist.

If somebody had attempted to explain to her what was what

before her flight from Fascist Italy and before her Soviet concentration camp experience do you think she would have begun to see the truth clearly? Do you think that she would have understood something which at that time was self-evident to the millions of concentration camp inmates and other Soviet citizens? I doubt it very much. That is why I have not been able to write you. Because it is not someone else's letters but one's own experiences that open one's eyes to the realities of this world.

However, to clear my own conscience and also because in the West a lot of people probably share your opinion, I will answer you. Here is the summary of the basic tenets of your two letters.

You begin by noting that in today's world there exist two socioeconomic systems, each having its own advantages and defects. You insist that the Communist system has at least *the advantage* of not experiencing the social decay observed in the West and, moreover, the ecological tragedy is less noticeable in the Communist countries. True, you acknowledge that the process of decay in the Communist countries is impeded not by ethical means but by political pressure. However, you undoubtedly regard as advantageous, in contrast to the West, the absence in these countries of pornography, advertising, drugs, gangsterism, and other elements of social decay. For you the Berlin Wall symbolizes the division of almost equally unjust worlds, and in your opinion, were Western society healthy there would have been no wall, and the West is no less guilty in its elevation than the East. Communism, according to you, is religion of the earthly life and has a deep justification, although its justification has been distorted. However, you are undecided whether this distortion is inherent only in the Soviet system or throughout the Communist world. In your opinion the West is headed toward catastrophe and can be saved only by a radical change of direction. You began your first letter with the explanation that you were writing to me because I, unlike other opposition writers from Communist countries, do not regard the West as the Promised Land; and you finished your second letter with the assertion that if I do not agree with you it would mean that each of us can see better the evil in his own society and finds it more difficult to understand somebody else's predicament.

First of all I do not know of any Samizdat writers (this term is better than "opposition writers") who are not aware of the evil existing in the West. Please name them for me. On the contrary, one is startled by the fact that men who have never been in the West, who were for decades cut off from every source of information about the West, even of the Communist slant, who day after day have been swept over with the flood of propaganda, could so realistically judge the capitalist world. Read the books of Nadezhda Mandelstam, Solzhenitsyn, Pomerantz, or any Samizdat writer and show me their illusions about the Western world. How could they have such illusions when the very presence of numerous Communist parties in the Western European countries, of the "New Left," of Western writers eulogizing the Communist system, and a lot of other things which the Soviet press is proudly broadcasting, indicate precisely that many things are wrong with the West. And at the same time, the opinions of people in the West—even those who are not Communists—about the East are quite often full of illusions and show a complete lack of understanding. Your own letters serve as an illustration of that fact.

What you are saying is this: There is the capitalist society and the Communist society. One is decaying and the other is kept from decay by political and police measures. But that is quite incorrect, dear Quadrelli, the whole point being that there is no society at all in the Communist countries. The essence of every totalitarianism, of every one-party dictatorship, is precisely the *alienation* of people. The *process of decay* which you see in Western society is *completely finished* in the Communist countries. Thus to see communism as a cure for social decay is like regarding death as the cure of a cancerous tumor.

Or let's take another comparison: In strict prisons there is no pornography, no advertising, no narcotics, no thieving; in a word, no decay. But there is also no society! This comparison can show nicely why people in Communist countries have no illusions about the West but nevertheless envy those living there, and when they have the chance, try to escape (which is the real reason why the Berlin Wall was erected), and at the same time, people living in the West have always distorted ideas about communism. Believe me, I spent several years in prison and I know first-hand that prisoners had no illusions about the life beyond the prison walls, but still they were always dreaming of freedom. And I know that those who have never been in prison always have a more or less incorrect idea about the life in prison.

A society exists where there is a free communication among people; where there is no free communication there is nothing decayed. One might even say that a society *is* free communication among free people and what you call the decay of the West indicates the presence of a growing number of inwardly *unfree* people, hence the decay. Communication among people is possible only as a contiguity of the depths of "I" of every man, that is, of the foundation of a person, the soul, of that spiritual beginning which does not belong to the visible physical reality. The alienation of a person from his fundamental "I" renders it impossible to communicate with another man. Freedom is precisely the unbroken bond with that "I." Why are there so many inwardly unfree men in relatively free societies? That is the basic problem you and I should ponder over. But in order to do this, one has first to understand that communism is the last stage of that very disease of separation, not its cure. And if the West is heading toward a catastrophe, it could suffer no worse fate than becoming totalitarian in the manner of Communist countries. One cannot make a man free by coercion, consequently it is not possible to heal society by one-party dictatorship.

Allow me to fortify my claims and simultaneously to illustrate the fact that people in Communist countries have no illusions whatever about the West, yet continue to thirst for it. I will do this by quoting a Samizdat author who is presently serving a fifteen-year sentence in a concentration camp for attempting to escape from behind (to put it symbolically) the "Berlin Wall."

> It appears that during the Fascists' rule, the Mafia ceased to exist. That, by the way, is to be expected. Every extremely dictatorial regime rather successfully deals with organized crime. Be it personal dictatorship, or dictatorship of administrative-party oligarchy, the regime regards organized crime as its own prerogative and will not stand for competition. One might even venture to express the somewhat paradoxical claim that the existence of organized crime serves—in any case for the time being—as an unmistakable indicator of democratic society. . . . Organized crime is the income tax for the blessings of democracy, its unavoidable expenses, just like pornography and many other things. It is either free press plus porno or *Pravda* minus porno. The efforts to diminish the expenses of democracy in the process not to be transformed into un-freedom is the eternal care of a democratic society.[1]

Communism is not, as you wrote, the religion of the earthly life. The Lord's Prayer, which European humanity has been reciting for twenty centuries, also speaks of "our daily bread" and about the Lord's kingdom "on Earth, as it is in Heaven." But communism wants to bring about that "Lord's Heaven on Earth" or the "Kingdom of Freedom," to use Marx's terminology, by force, by oppression, by the "dictatorship of the proletariat," that is, by the dictatorship of that "avant-garde of proletarians"—the Communist Party. And that means by the abolition of freedom, by the absolute power of the party, and by the alienation of man from his "I," and finally by the death of society.

The question is not of the goal but of the means of achieving it. That is why it does not matter what communism we are talking about—Soviet, Chinese, Cuban, or possibly Italian. Where there is political-spiritual monopoly there is death of society, no matter what idea stands behind the dictatorship and monopoly being established. Do you really think that there are presently no concentration camps with millions and tens of millions of prisoners in China? Point out to me any phenomenon in present-day China that did not exist in Stalin's USSR.

And now about "ecological tragedy." I hope you will agree with me that human thought, human spirit, is much more precious than, for instance, parts of the human body. I don't think I am wrong in assuming that you would prefer to be without legs than to be an idiot. And so when everything that represents the spiritual essence of a man is daily being mercilessly destroyed on one half of our planet, as is happening in totalitarian Communist countries, to regard as a tragedy the destruction of flora and fauna (which, of course, in itself is not a cheerful phenomenon) is, to cite a Russian proverb, "to mourn the hair after the head is cut off."

Besides, you evidently do not read Soviet newspapers and are consequently uninformed about the heedless destruction of woods, the total annihilation of fish in the rivers of the Soviet industrial regions, and the pollution of even the Baikal, the deepest lake in the world. The ecological problem is connected to our technical-industrial culture and not to our social systems. It can be solved only in a democratic society, because in totalitarian countries, the only thing that could solve the problem—the human spirit—is crushed. I cannot avoid the temptation to quote Kuznetsov again: "The persecution of dissidents is more terrible than genocide, which takes human life; but destruction of dissent infringes the spirit, which is the very essence of . . . life."[2]

If all the fish living in the Mediterranean were destroyed, that would be *a lesser tragedy* than the introduction of a one-party totalitarian system in Italy. The recreation of life in the sea merely involves great technical difficulties, while the recreation of life of a society and the liquidation of a one-party monopoly is a task which has never yet been achieved anywhere. (This is why it is so tragic to see the reintroduction of the dogmatic Marxist conformity of ideas in all the spheres of life in Yugoslavia, the country that for years has been not only economically but also spiritually the least totalitarian of all the Communist countries.)

This seems to be all that I wanted to tell you. But you may still conclude after my answer that the evil in one's own society is understandable and that in somebody else's is not. Before doing that, however, try at least to compare the following facts: It is possible for you and every Italian to express your opinions, even publicly, in the press (be it liberal, Communist, Christian, Rightist, etc.) and it is impossible for me and all the millions of inhabitants of Communist countries to express any opinions other than the one proclaimed by the last Party Congress or plenary session. For you as a writer this should be a crucial question. Not to mention such liberties inaccessible to me as the possibility of traveling abroad, reading books and newspapers one chooses, taking part in political and religious organizations, and many, many other things, including such trifles as being able to buy items for personal use. (Even Yugoslavs still travel to Tieste to shop; and it is easy to do so, since here, in contrast with other socialist countries, the passport is refused only to the open dissidents. Yugoslavia is, in the words of visiting Czechs, a "real America.") But those are, of course, trifles.

Try to think over the meaning of these facts. Only then can you say that every society has its own evil, and its own advantages. Social evil is common, but this fact is felt, it seems, only by people in Communist countries. This is their only advantage.

Respectfully yours,
Mihajlo Mihajlov

Novi Sad, 1973

NOTES

1. Eduard Kuznetsov, *Diaries,* published by Editeurs Reunis, Paris, 1973, pp. 52-53.
2. Ibid., p. 64.

Dostoyevsky On The Catholic "Left"

The negative attitude of the great Russian writer toward the Roman Catholic Church was based on his opinion that the powerful historical organization headed by the Pope, who had supreme authority in the affairs of religion and consequently of the salvation of the human soul, had illegally seized "the power of the keys" *(potestas clavium)*; that is, the power to bind and to make decisions. Thus the church took away from millions and millions of believers the freedom of conscience; and, since in Christianity salvation is conceived exclusively in freedom, this meant the church had robbed the people of the possibility of salvation. Such an appraisal of the Catholic Church was expressed by Dostoyevsky most forcefully in the legend of "The Grand Inquisitor," told by a hero in his novel *The Brothers Karamazov.*

The originality and depth of that story is in the fact that the Grand Inquisitor was not a mercenary, power-craving man (as Catholic priests were depicted in the rationalistic thought of the French Enlightenment), but actually a martyr, who out of *love* toward men was taking away their freedom and putting all the responsibility on his own shoulders. He was convinced that man is too weak to bear the burden of freedom, a burden making man responsible for all his actions, responsible for the salvation or the eternal damnation of his soul, and thus endlessly miserable. The genius of Dostoyevsky is that his dialectics revealed the roots of such an attitude toward men: deep down the Grand Inquisitor *did not believe* in Christ and did not believe that in every man there is a grain of freedom and immortality (expressed in the language of the Bible—"Man is created in God's image"); he therefore regarded it as indispensable to organize life on earth under the absolute authority of the church. This prompted Dostoyevsky to state in one of his articles that love toward men, but love without belief in God, very naturally leads to the greatest coercion over men and turns their lives completely into hell on earth. Dostoyevsky expressed this thought in his formula: "God is love, but one can't say that love is God."

In his attitude toward the Catholic Church and his opinion that its basic moving force is *disbelief* in Christ, Dostoyevsky is for the most part only following Luther. But he was almost certainly the first one to express, for the nineteenth century a completely paradoxical thought, that the Catholic Church and the militant Communist movement, which was springing up at that time, were phenomena of the same spiritual nature, and that in the future they were bound to merge. The only difference between them, as he saw it, was that the Catholic Church was a vested unbelief, and the Communist movement an open atheism.

In his little-known article in the journal *Citizen* (no. 41, 1873), Dostoyevsky expressed the following thoughts, which are very interesting for our time:

> The Pope will succeed in swaying the people by walking barefoot, naked as a beggar, with an army of twenty-thousand Jesuits experienced in capturing human souls. Can Karl Marx and Bakunin resist these fighters? Hardly; Catholicism is skilled in making concessions where they are needed and in reconciling all. And what does it take to convince ignorant and beggarly people that communism is that very Christianity and that Christ was talking only about just that. . . . All these interpreters of human nature and psychologists rush to the people and bring them a new Christ, who is agreeable to everything, a Christ proclaimed at the last impious council in Rome. . . . Yes, our friends and brothers—the Jesuits will say—all that you take the trouble to do, all this we already have had for you in this book for a long time, and your leaders have stolen all that from us. . . . Before, the main strength of faith was in humbleness,

but its end has come, and the Pope has authority to abolish it, for his power is limitless. Yes, you are all brothers and Christ himself ordered everybody to be brothers; and if your older brothers do not want to have you in their homes as brothers, then take sticks and penetrate their homes and force them to be your brothers. Christ waited a long time for your corrupted older brothers to repent, and now he himself has allowed us to proclaim *"Fraternité ou la mort."* . . .

Those words are smooth-tongued but undoubtedly the populace will accept the proposition: they will discern in the unexpected ally a great unifying force, consenting to everything and not hindering anything, a power real and historical. And on top of everything, they are given faith again. Thus the hearts of too many people will be appeased for too many of them have long felt a loneliness without God.

Startling words written a hundred years ago! At the present time, when the Catholic "left" is growing in the West, when priest-terrorists appear in Latin America, when Jesuit fathers travel more and more often to Moscow, when Catholic theologians are persistently trying somehow to reconcile Christianity and Marxism ideologically, it is really worthwhile to analyze the question: Where does the road foreseen by Dostoyevsky lead the Catholic Church and the entire Western Christian world (if one can use this expression at all in our times)? And what is awaiting mankind at the end of that road?

This question is much more interesting because in the Communist countries a religious rebirth, already noticeable to anyone who wants to see it, is moving in precisely the *opposite* direction. This was symbolically expressed in the sharpest way in *Thoughts at Random* by the extremely talented Samizdat writer Synavsky-Tertz: "Enough talking about man, it is time to talk about God."

From a social-historical perspective the Catholic Church undoubtedly is not connected with the capitalist social order. It existed in both slave-owning and feudal societies. And theoretically there are no obstacles to its activity within a socialist order if we regard socialism exclusively as a form of economic-judicial social order in which the means of production are not privately owned. That is why the support given by the Catholic Church until very recently to strongly capitalist and even undemocratic, authoritarian regimes says much about the spiritual stagnation which could one day cause the Vatican to compromise with and support the totalitarian-Communist regimes.

The progenitor of the very word "socialism," Saint-Simon, conceived a direct link between Christianity and socialism in his book *New Christianity;* and the founder of French communism, Cabet, in his book *Genuine Christianity* insisted that nobody can call himself a Christian if he is not a Communist. [1] Why then did Marx and especially Lenin lead such an uncompromising struggle not only against the church (which would be in a way understandable since the church, both Catholic and Orthodox, was at that time tied up with the capitalist system), but especially against Christianity, against every religion per se, against the belief in God, transcendentality, and the immortality of the soul? Why didn't they proclaim after Saint-Simon and Cabet that God is on their side and that the New Testament calls for realization of the just socialist society? To answer that question would be to answer the basic question of our time; it would require an explanation of why the religious rebirth in the Communist countries is not only anti-Marxist but often also anticlerical; and it would also require an answer as to why Dostoyevsky—after penetrating the spiritual depths from which the ideas he perceived surfaced into life one whole century later—had such an aversion to the prospect of a possible transition of the Catholic Church to the ideological perspective of the Communist movement.

The issue here is not the socialization of the means of production. Such a socialization per se is not connected with revolutionary violence, atheism, or Communist dictatorship. The issue also is not in the Marxist theory about historical development, according to which the development allegedly depends completely on the class struggle. The issue is not even in the basic theoretical premise of Marxism that the "base," that is, society, determines the "consciousness," that is, the spiritual sphere; according to that tenet, in a classless socialist society, man's alienation, most strongly expressed in religion, which is in turn a part of the "superstructure" over the exploitive class society, will end, because the "need for God" (allegedly only a self-projection of the unfree alienated man) will pass away for good. That very theoretical tenet is itself a consequence of something else, and if actually the whole controversial issue consisted of "base" (society) and "superstructure" (spiritual sphere), Marxism would have no particular reason for such a bloody battle with "projections and mirages." If it were true the "superstructure" would have collapsed with the change of the "base."

Why then does Marxism find it so necessary to completely negate the transcendentality, the spiritual sphere, heaven and soul? If the socialist social order were conceived only as a more justly organized society in the socioeconomic sphere, then there would be no need to negate the ontological reality of the spiritual sphere. However, the moving force of Marxian communism is the belief that it can bring about the realization of no less than heaven on earth (in the words of Marx the "kingdom of freedom"). *The main thing* in this belief is the conviction that the "kingdom of freedom" can be brought about only by force, by the revolutionary dictatorship of that class (or rather its avant-garde—the party), which, according to Marx, is historically predestined to annihilate not only its own position as an exploited class, but also exploitation in general, consequently bringing freedom to itself and all mankind. This insistence on *the necessity of violence* as the only instrument for the realization of the "kingdom of freedom" is the essence of revolutionary Marxism.

Thus, the basis of everything is the struggle against freedom, which intrinsically resists any suppression and thus stands in the way of the creation of the "kingdom of freedom." If there exists a spiritual sphere invisible for human eyes (including all kinds of physical and technical instruments) then man does not depend completely on external, visible reality and he is a creature ontologically free in relation to this world. Therefore, the forcible alteration of this world does not affect basic human spiritual depths, and the possibility of a heaven on earth becomes questionable.

If, however, there is no spirit and soul, if God is only a fiction and a result of the alienation of the inherent essence of man himself, brought about by the unjust class society, then the violence whose objective is to "cure the alienation" of the foolish man is well justified. The Marxists take it as a *self-evident fact* that there is no spiritual sphere whatsoever, and their theory of "base and superstructure" is only a consequence of the fact. But since in the everyday practice of building communism, Marxists repeatedly clash with actions and deeds which definitely do not depend on "base" but are dictated by the allegedly nonexisting spiritual sphere, they are forced to explain it by the "ill will" of man or by the schemes of the class enemy, and they punish these deeds mercilessly.

This attraction to a mandatory salvation of mankind is witness to *an already occurred alienation* from the spiritual sphere, a bedazzlement and loss of touch with the roots of life. This alienation is deeply connected with the whole scientific-technical spirit of our epoch and is only evidence of the forceful intrusion into human life of the completely man-made, mechanical world in the place of nature.

The authorities, as the instigators of this mandatory building of the "kingdom of freedom," predetermine a political dictatorship and the annihilation of any manifestation of man's freedom. Love toward men without faith in God becomes aspiration toward power and the power destroys all love. Every forceful improvement of life turns out to be hell on earth.

Nowhere has the link between Christianity and freedom stood out so clearly as in the confrontation between communism and Christianity. If Christ is reality, if freedom is instilled in every human being, then the violence is not justified. Then any kind of violence and coercion is a fight against God.

At the same time, one of the strongest arguments in favor of revolutionary violence is a claim that the violence is only an inevitable means of stopping the everyday violence of an exploitive society, and that in such an unjust society, a sermon in church calling for resignation only supports the oppression and serves to prolong the hell on earth. The premise of this claim is that one resists violence only with violence. If one renounces violence in his struggle with evil then it is completely falsely interpreted as "non-resistance" to evil. (The church has really been violating the truth through almost all of its history with its preaching of nonresistance to the social evil.) The above-mentioned premise is untrue because the very history of the first centuries of Christianity is an example of the uncompromising, sacrificial, and consistent resistance of Christians to the attempt of the powerful Roman Emporium to inaugurate absolute power encompassing the spiritual sphere, i.e., religion. That Christian resistance ended in victory, although violence was not used in opposing violence. And vice versa, history shows countless examples of violence used to oppose violence and evil used to fight evil, breeding endless evil on earth.

The temptation of worldly power, that third temptation of Christ in the desert, has always been an invisible fellow traveler on the road traveled by the Catholic Church. Only the spirit of the forceful organization of human society, the idea of salvation by force, could have given birth to the stakes of the Inquisition, the index of forbidden books, the Jesuit state in Paraguay, and many things that caused the almost total loss of faith in God by contemporary mankind. Now, when power which overtly worships violence as its supreme value has been established on half the globe, that eternal temptation to the Catholic Church has become unbearably strong. It pushes the church to find ways to approach the emerging world, and the prophetic vision of Dostoyevsky is becoming horrifyingly real. Moreover, the Vatican is hypnotized by the same illusion the whole West is subjected to, and fails to discern that, after half a century, in Russia and Eastern Europe Marxism is spiritually dead.

The Catholic Church faces at the present time the choice of either finding a common language with the Communist movement and giving its blessings to the forceful building of heaven on earth, or taking sides with Solzhenitsyn, Synavsky, Nadezhda Mandelstam, and the whole anti-Marxist religious renaissance.

The whole history of the Catholic Church predestines it toward the usual historical blunder. But this time the mistake might be the last one. Because on one hand the anti-Marxist spiritual rebirth will, in that case, be directed not only against the Communist rule, but also against the church. On the other hand, if the religious rebirth does not overcome the power of totalitarian slavery, then after a period of tolerance toward the church which gave its blessings to dictatorship, there will inevitably come a movement when the overt atheism will sweep out of existence the hidden atheism. That would mean the end of Catholic Christianity, if not all historical Christianity.

But to side with Solzhenitsyn and others means to overcome the terrible temptation of worldy power, which for too many people became identified with the Catholic Church itself. Will the church, in which over the centuries has appeared not only Torquemada but also Francis of Assisi, be able to muster enough faith not to come to an agreement (or even worse to compete) with the strongest and most absolute worldly power ever to appear on the face of the earth? The world conquest by that power would mean the end of the life of mankind, since there is life only where there is freedom.

Novi Sad, 1973

NOTES

1. From the article by Zennkovsky entitled, "Insensitive as a Nova" which appeared in the publication *Orthodox Thought,* no. 3.

Answers to Ten Questions of Mr. K. D. Pomerantzev for Russian Thought*

QUESTION: The Soviet Communist experiment brought a lot of misery, evil, and suffering to the Russian people. Don't you think that it also brought some positive results? If so, then what are those positive results?

ANSWER: If we are talking about external, visible results of a half-century of Communist Party power in Russia—that is, about industrialization, science, technology, economy, culture, art, standard of living, education, social customs, social ideas—then I maintain that, contrary to the firmly held opinion in the West and the claims of Soviet propaganda, the results of that half-century of experience are extremely negative. They are negative even if one writes off the victims of concentration camps and bloody purges, organized famine and collectivization, on account of "personality cult" and the "pangs of growth." However, the experience of misery and suffering, no matter how terrible and painful, does remove the film of spiritual blindness from one's eyes and opens up the possibility for spiritual rebirth, which is a precondition for all renaissance. The greatest positive result of the Communist experiment, I believe, is that the Communist idea, Marxism, and the materialistic philosophy and Weltanschauung no longer exist in a spiritual sense in Russia (in contrast to the West).

They do, of course, exist in everyday life, in thousands of books, newspapers, and propaganda materials, in resolutions and party meetings, and especially in the activity of the KGB

*Russian social-philosophical and literary publication in Paris—TRANS.

(Soviet Secret Police). But in a spiritual sense communism, Marxism, and materialism are dead. And dead for good, at that. The type of people who actively supported dictatorship and who believed in the "just cause" of communism have been replaced by the type of people who no longer believe in the common good brought about by the forced organization of society, but who nevertheless believe in the invincibility of power and violence. But that is already an immense change in the social consciousness of people because it proves that the idea of Communist dictatorship has lost its moral justification for silencing the voice of conscience. One must be a Marxist and believe that the "social existence determines the social consciousness" or an American "behaviorist" to despair that the social existence in Russia is still a Communist one. I have no doubt that a new, post-Communist consciousness is being born (I call it "planetary" consciousness because of its significance for the world and for all mankind). It is arising now among only a small number of people who are trying to give meaning to the experience they have lived through, but the beginning of everything significant is always small. The basic elements of this consciousness are already present. They can be noticed in the persistently recurring thoughts in the works of Samizdat writers, especially Nadezhda Mandelstam, Snyavsky, and Solzhenitsyn. I do not know if readers in the West have noticed that Nadezhda Mandelstam and Solzhenitsyn call these fundamental positions of the new consciousness, resulting from a comprehension of their experiences, "laws." Contemporary science does not know such "laws," but it seems that science will have to be altered.

Here is this basic "law" in the words of N. Mandelstam: "A human sliver, even the most mediocre one, has a mysterious talent to 'turn the stream.' "[1] "The inner life, more likely determines to a great degree external events than vice versa."[2] "Hope has a special characteristic; it comes true if it is preserved."[3] Solzhenitsyn in his *First Circle,* talks openly, I believe, about the "law" which led the principal hero of the novel, Nerzhin, into the "sharshka" (prison for scientists-TRANS.), where he was able to fulfill his need to see and realize what was happening, which was his deepest inclination in life. Solzhenitsyn wrote, "Our wishes come true without fail if they are genuinely strong."

The realization that there is *an indissoluble connection* between the inner world of man (his soul, not his consciousness) and the external world, and that the inner world completely *determines* the destiny and all the events in man's personal life in the external world—that realization is the basic paradoxical assertion of the new spiritual experience. It is paradoxical because, from a superficial view, the destiny of an individual was determined totally by the mighty totalitarian pressure of the external world. But those who have lived through and survived the sinister experience of totalitarian society constantly insist that the paradoxical, even mystical, "law" is an obvious fact. And from that basic "law" stem other "laws" of the new consciousness: "the law of self-destruction of evil" in the words of N. Mandelstam. That law was confirmed by the bloody historical experience of the Soviet purges, when every new wave of terror destroyed the cohorts of yesterday's executioners. The other law was expressed in a deep attraction to nonexistence and an inner renunciation of freedom, which logically led millions of people first toward absolute conformity in thinking and later toward death in concentration camps. This makes understandable the claims of the Samizdat writers that all historical determinism is a lie; that it is not society which determines a person, but vice versa; that to be a slave is not a misfortune but a terrible sin; that there were no innocent victims; that a man who was bereaved of everything is becoming free again (Solzhenitsyn's thought); and that "the feeling of sinfulness is the basic 'wealth of man' " (again in the words of N. Mandelstam) because the awareness of the actual responsibility for one's own destiny and that of others is precisely what makes a man spiritually free and brings him back in touch with life.

All this leads to the fundamental idea, still timidly expressed by the Samizdat writers (the church Samizdat is a different matter, and I will explain why I don't regard it as an especially significant phenomenon in my answer to question no. 9), the idea which Dostoyevsky regarded as absolutely indispensable for man to have any kind of conscious life. That idea is, to put it more exactly, faith in the indestructibility of the human soul. As the experience of the Samizdat writers shows, it is on the soul that our fate and the existence of the world depends, and not vice versa (as some would want us to believe).

On this faith depends not only the life of a society but even the cancerous tumors, as witnessed by M. Beck in his *New Assignment,* and many others. The new consciousness will undoubtedly bring about a revision of not just the humanities but science in general, because the basic premise of science is the dogma that the laws of the universe do not depend on the human soul and its ontological freedom. Thus, in my opinion, this incredible spiritual revolution, whose first shoots are presently beginning to appear, is definitely a positive, if indeed completely unexpected, result of the Russian revolution. The changes in the human consciousness, which the spiritual revolution is bound to provoke in the future, are going to usher in a new historical era. In this sense one has to compare the role of Russian emigration (and generally emigration from all totalitarian countries) with the role played by Jewish exiles in the first centuries of Christianity.

QUESTION: Is not Stalinism only a natural continuation of Leninism?

ANSWER: Of course, there is no question about it. Even the Marxists, as for instance the prominent Yugoslav group around the magazine *Praxis*, disown Lenin, although they still worship Marx, admittedly the "young Marx." Although the connection between Lenin and Stalin is becoming persuasively evident (because it is impossible to point at anything in the practice of Stalin which had not already been conceived by Lenin), the connection between Marx and Stalinism has not as yet been realized. The decisive role in realizing that link in the future will be played by the remarkable Russian thinkers of the twentieth century: Shestov, Berdyaev, Frank, Lossky, Boulgakov, and others. Their books will give and are already giving enormous help in the creation of the new consciousness, the post-Communist one, which they have foreseen in many ways, although they did not see its *final form*. I would like to emphasize that the post-Communist consciousness is not the same as the anti-Communist consciousness, which the West knows. Between the people who lived through communism (actively or passively) and who have given meaning to that terrifying experience, and those who lived all their lives in democratic countries (to be an emigrant is a special category, because emigration is also a kind of camp or exile), there is always an invisible but impenetrable wall of incomprehension, even when the people find themselves to be of the same ideological position. Communism is terrifying, and prison is terrifying, but not in the sense that those who did not experience them fear them. They are terrifying because of something else, so powerfully described by Solzhenitsyn in his *First Circle*. (They break the spirit—Trans.) That is why I agree with the Italian writer, Ignazio Silone, who expressed the thought somewhere in his writings that communism could be conquered only by those who personally endured it.

QUESTION: Is the liberalization of the Soviet regime possible in your opinion, and if so, then to what degree?

ANSWER: If by liberalization you mean the weakening of suppression in some or even all the spheres of social life in the

USSR (although one can talk only conditionally about society in totalitarian countries, because the essence of totalitarianism is the *disassociation* of men), then such a liberalization is not only possible but has periodically occurred since the October revolution. For example, the period of NEP (New Economic Policy) was the first liberalization, then came a short period after Stalin's "dizziness from success," then a period during the Second World War, then after the death of Stalin, after the address of Khrushchev at the Twentieth Party Congress and again after the Twenty-second Congress. Such a liberalization has a limit and that is the monopoly of the political power of the party. Yugoslavia is a country where the Communist Party reached the very limit of the possible Communist liberalization. One more step and there would have been a democratization which would have meant the end of the political monopoly of the party but not of socialism. Unfortunately, the party started in time to regress. As long as there is political monopoly in socialist countries, every liberalization will be followed by a new suppression, and there is no guarantee whatsoever that the next suppression will be less terrible than the previous one.

QUESTION: Do you think that communism in the USSR will be gradually overcome (evolution) or overthrown (revolution)?

ANSWER: I think that it is necessary to take into account three unquestionable facts when discussing the possibility of the end of Communist dictatorship in Russia. First, the Soviet system has not evolved in its half-century of existence, and theoretically it cannot happen, since all the changes have just been periodical waves of suppression and liberalization. Second, no totalitarian system in history has ever been overcome from within. For that to happen would require a miracle similar to a spontaneous cure of the cancerous tumor. Third, if by revolution one means an armed uprising, then on one hand, such a thing is inconceivable in a totalitarian regime, and especially in a time of peace; on the other hand, it was the Communist experiment itself that greatly alienated the people from violence, which is more or less innate in every political revolution. But at the same time, what would you call the appearance of the Samizdat on such a massive scale, a new spiritual consciousness, of hundreds of heroic sacrifices doomed to end in the camp and in psycho-prisons? That is a genuine revolution, but one that does not "break the continuity of times" as the Communist revolutions do. On the contrary, it is one that restores this link. (By the way, the experiences of the Samizdat writers will also bring changes in our notions about the flow of time. Have you noticed how the time "stops" when a man gets into prison [Solzhenitsyn] or how seconds last for an eternity when one is awaiting arrest [Mandelstam]? There is hope that soon we will begin to accept and understand such words from the Apocalypse as that there will be first "half-time," then "quarter-time," and then "there will be no time at all." For prison is a "divarication," the breaking of the continuity of time, when there is only frozen, dead, endless time. ["Half-time" is already a road to freedom.]) Thus the process of liberation of Russia I conceive as more similar to the struggle and victory of Christianity in the Roman emporium than the result of the activities of Socialist Revolutionaries. (Socialist Revolutionaries were a political party in prerevolutionary Russia—Trans.). In that sense it is hard to overestimate the importance of the Committee for Human Rights headed by Sakharov and Chalidze. The growing awareness of legal processes and demands for legality are the foundation stones of an ideological and political struggle with a totalitarian dictatorship, which even in theory (as conceived and expressed by Lenin) is the negation of legality.

Of course, one cannot exclude the possibility of riots and unexpected unrests, which would hardly speed the end of dictatorship, but could hasten the process of overcoming totalitarianism internally. Pacifists in the West who dream about a stable peace "all over the world" and who, at the same time, do not want to interfere with the "internal affairs" of the totalitarian countries would have to take into account a paradoxical claim which was first expressed by Pasternak in his *Doctor Zhivago* and then by N. Mandelstam, Anna Akhmatova and others, that the Second World War, with all its cruelties and terrors, brought an inner *relief* to the people in the Soviet Union. The war period was the only *bright* period during the absolute rule of Stalin, because it "saved [us] from the schism which is so characteristic of our lives in the time of peace."[4] The importance of that evidence has not yet been understood and evaluated. There are no more "internal (personal) affairs" on our planet at all, and there cannot be; which, by the way, does not mean that I stand for the "Cold War." On the contrary, the expansion of trade connections and the increase of contacts with the captive world open up great possibilities for truthful information, which is the most dangerous enemy of party monopoly. And at the same time such contacts are a wonderful cure for many naive people in the West, who sincerely want to know the truth.

QUESTION: Is it desirable that the Communist dictatorship in the USSR be replaced by a democratic system of the Western type?

ANSWER: If by the democratic system of the Western type you mean the legal organization of society, which guarantees freedom of speech, political and labor organizations, freedom of assembly, freedom of the press, freedom of religious beliefs, and freedom of economic enterprise—then such a system is not only desirable but the only possible one after the expected recovery of totalitarian societies, because totalitarianism is overcome only where there is spiritual liberalization, which is the basis of the democratic system.

However, if by the "Western type" you mean the contemporary organization of economic and political life in the West, the private ownership of means of production, i. e., capitalism or neocapitalism, then, in my opinion, such a road for the post-Communist societies is both impossible and undesirable. Socialization of the economic life is going on in different forms all over the world, and the center of gravity of the question about freedom and slavery (and that means the question of life or death for humanity) shifts completely into the sphere of political organization of society. Thus the questions of economic ownership lose their priority. The democratic system is only historically linked with capitalism, just as the totalitarian system is linked with socialism. The possibilities for democracy in a socialist society (but not one-party, of course) are much greater than in a capitalist society. One must not forget that all the ills of the totalitarian system originated in capitalism and were only completely developed in Communist society. Take for example the creation of huge industrial and trade monopolies, the religious indifference, the loss of values in personal and social life, the blind faith in progress and the omnipotence of science, the total negation of man's freedom (how about the books of such Western scientists as the American psychologist Skinner and the French biologist Monnot?) and a lot of other things that are a real warning that the West might fall into an Orwellian world.

QUESTION: What Soviet writers (excluding Solzhenitsyn) do you regard as most promising?

ANSWER: I have a feeling that the heyday of the first Samizdat writers is ending. For the last ten years Russian literature has completely changed; however, the most talented writers, Solzhenitsyn, Mandelstam, Snyavsky, and also Okudzhava and Pomerantz, are not young people any more, and what they have written has been nurtured for decades. It is impossible to overestimate their work, and I even cannot avoid the temptation to proclaim that in our time only Russian thought, only Russian Samizdat literature, is genuinely meaningful in our world.

Take, for instance, in comparison with the memoirs of N. Mandelstam, such a brilliantly written, but artificial book as the *Antimemoirs* of Malraux! And Malraux is not at all a superficial man, but still he is so far from having the spiritual depth and power of observation of that wisest of women! That is who should receive the Nobel Prize!

But nevertheless, it is hard to talk about "the most promising writers." They cannot be seen. The most brilliant young literary figures are either in prison, in psycho-prison, or abroad. The wave of Samizdat brought forth the spiritual treasures that were stored for decades, but there is still no normal growth and development in Russian literature. In all probability we are at the threshold of a new period of suppression by the authorities, during which not only tens and hundreds, but thousands and thousands of people will learn spiritual experience and the new consciousness which has manifested itself in Samizdat works of the past. And the result of that hidden process will become apparent only during the next thaw. But the allotted time will come, maybe much earlier than we now think. . . .

QUESTION: How do you explain the appearance of "left-wing communism"?

ANSWER: The reasons for the appearance of "left-wing Communist" tendencies are the same as the reasons for the appearance of all the totalitarian movements in our century, be they Soviet and Chinese communism, German national-socialism, Italian fascism, etc. They are the same illness, but it takes on different forms and different degrees of tension, depending on national spirit and historical traditions. The root of the illness is in the alienation of man from the depths of his own spirit (schism) and consequently from actual live contact with his fellowmen. The unbearable loneliness and loss of purpose in life that alienation brings force one to tread the road of the imaginary (following not basic, but external, secondary realities), that is, one seeks the unification with other people on basis of an idea, be it racial, class, or national. The law of genuine spirituality is replaced willy-nilly by a pseudo-spirituality; and in a world where there is no Francis of Assisi or Sergius of Radonezh (Russian saint—TRANS.), of course contemporary man must see even Che Guevara as a hero.

We know quite well what that all leads to, but unfortunately we still do not know if there is a less painful cure than the one experienced by the Russian people. (Try to shove "left-wing communism" onto Russia!) That is the basic question on which depends the destiny of the West. The role played by the contemporary spiritless industrial culture, and especially by the faith in the omnipotency of science, natural-historical determinism, and progress in the appearance of that illness, that is, in the causes of alienation, is another question. Our whole civilization is in many ways the *consequence* of an isolation from the depths of life. The very "freedom *from*" and lack of "purpose" that the youth in the West are so fed up with show that there is no longer real freedom, that is, the inner contact with the spirit. (Even in the plays of Samuel Beckett time stands frozen on zero.) That is why totalitarianism, replacing the useless "freedom from," is only an external consequence of the inner slavery.

That the "New Left" is inspired by Mao's China and not by the "revisionist" USSR, is completely natural and shows that the climate in which totalitarianism develops is a sickness of spirit, a thirst for self-destruction that N. Mandelstam writes about. It seems that this illness is only gathering its strength in the West. The extreme radicalism of the Chinese Communist Party, its fanaticism and pseudoreligiosity are certainly stronger centers of attraction than the post-Stalinist Russia, with its loss of faith in communism. It is to the historical traditions of Russia ("Moscow tzars") that both "left-wing" and "right-wing" Communists ascribe all the sins of the Communist dictatorship. "Left-wing" Communists evidently maintain that historical China in comparison with Russia was a democratic state; while the "Right-Wing" Western and revisionist Communists seem to forget that, for instance, the short period of dictatorship of the Jacobins bloodied the cultural capital of the world in a totally Leninist-Stalinist way. The first symptom of the spiritual blindness of our contemporaries is their unwillingness to see that dictatorship per se, no matter what the ideas, people, and principles behind it, leads right to the death of society.

Although it is true that the era of totalitarianism started with a Russian called Vladimir Ulyanov—Lenin—and Russians feel shame because the killer on such a global scale appeared among the Russian people—nevertheless that shame is diminished by the fact that the worship of Lenin and "revolutionary violence" is characteristic of those very people in other nations who ascribe the "failure of communism" in Russia to the Russian historical tradition.

QUESTION: Is "self-management" possible in highly developed countries?

ANSWER: It depends on your definition of self-management. The present popularity of this very word means that it is becoming a word-symbol, like the words revolution, freedom, brotherhood, equality. All those words always express some deep aspiration of men, but in the process of their implementation into life, they often lead to the opposite results.

That is why it is very important to make clear what the issue is in the actual realization of self-management. Nowadays, especially for socialists in the West, self-management means the idea of a free society in the production-economic sphere, that is, workers working in an enterprise, who are the owners of it, who are managing the production, profit, "surplus value," investment, according to their own judgment. I have to emphasize that this concept of self-management is, in the best sense, thoughtless, and in the worst sense, a demagoguery; this is so because of the Marxist dogma that politics is allegedly only a "superstructure over production relations."

First of all, the concept of "self-management" does not say anything about the political organization of society as a whole. It does not say how to avoid the problems anticipated by G. P. Fedotov (expressed in his remarkable book *Christian in the Revolution*), who claims that "struggle between cooperatives is no less terrible than the struggle of personal owners." The Yugoslav experiment also proves his point.

Second, such a concept of self-management does not say anything about the organization of power and management itself, in the enterprises; thus the political question is again left out. Monopoly by one group is as much a possibility in a factory as in a multimillion populated country, where all the laborers are also "owners" of all the means of production.

Third, our industrial culture is becoming so unified and interdependent on its component parts that a stoppage or just a slowdown in the works of one factory provokes a paralysis of tens and even hundreds of other industrial businesses. Thus, one cannot talk about any self-management in the sphere of production; and the solution of all questions, even technological ones, shifts into the political sphere. Using again the words of Mr. Fedotov: "Although in our 'materialistic' era economic powers are very strong, they are still subject to the political powers."

If the idea, expressed once by Khrushchev (I don't know for what purpose), about the possibility of division of the Communist Party of the Soviet Union into two parts (an agrarian and an industrial) had actually come true, its meaning for the democratization of socialist countries would have been incomparably more important than hundreds of Yugoslav one-party self-managing brands of socialism. This is simply because the realization of that idea would have led to the complete liquidation of political monopoly in the country.

The idea of self-management can have some actual importance only if it means *political* self-management, political democracy. In the West, political democracy is limited by the economic power of the big capitalist monopolies and military-industrial complexes, and in the East, by the dictatorship of the Communist Party. Of course, the question of to what degree our technical-industrial culture per se enslaves a man (even in the most favorable economic-political democracy) is a completely different matter. That issue brings us back to your first question, to that already growing revolution of the "planetary" consciousness, to the religious rebirth. And the religious rebirth, if I am not completely deceived, will in turn change the goals and the direction of the development of our culture, to such a degree that our present questions, worries, ideological and sociopolitical aspirations will lose all sense. In a similar fashion contemporary psychology loses all its sense compared to parapsychology. I am writing about all these issues in my book "Unscientific Thoughts," which I have been working on for four years now. However, I do not want to express the ideas and thoughts which are the basis of that book prematurely and in bits and pieces.

QUESTION: Do you think communism can be opposed only by a revived Christianity, which will no longer be a "private matter" (the idea of N. Berdyaev)?

ANSWER: I believe that I have already, in a sense, answered your question; but I have to add that Christianity has never been a "private matter." And I mean in both the positive sense, when Christianity meant the victory over death of every living thing in the universe (in Solzhenitsyn's words death is the final alienation, "eternal exile") and in the negative sense, when it meant the historical, very human activity of the churches, activity which brought about, in a way quite naturally, the Holy Inquisition. The negation of existence of "private matters" shows the pseudoreligious character of every kind of totalitarianism. And that very pseudoreligiousness attracts the youth of a *religiousless* world, the world where there are only "private matters" (or the "freedom from").

I am not at all convinced that the presently existing churches, including Soviet underground churches, will play an important part in the forthcoming religious rebirth. The Christian sermon in a pagan world was an easy thing compared to the religious sermon in the contemporary world (both Western and Eastern), because even the very idea of the Almighty Creator of Heaven and Earth and the concepts of sin and salvation, of hell and paradise, have become completely incomprehensible in a world which has pseudoscientific faith in cosmic determinism. It was easy for the apostle Paul in Athens to proclaim that "the unknown God" was Jesus Christ. The Greeks had a definite conception of their gods as omnipotent conscious powers, directing human destinies. And we are stuck only with eternal laws of nature and matter, that have indifference toward men. The idea of soul, let alone immortal soul, a serious man is not even supposed to mention.

Churches are using words long ago forgotten; and even the stories of the New Testament, with their deep spiritual revelations expressed in a simple language that illiterate shepherds in Palestine could understand, will soon become quite abstract and incomprehensible and will require great preparatory learning for the generations brought up in big cities, never having a chance to see a live lamb or grapevine, to understand them. And that goes for church services and rituals even more. I am ashamed, but I have to admit that I, for one, have several times examined the meaning and symbolism behind the church service, only to forget it again later on, just as I have forgotten the meaning of many terms in Hindu philosophy. There was a time when even the most uneducated man could understand the language of the Christian church.

However, *a new language for the old Book of Revelation* began to shine through in the works of Samizdat writers. I think it had already begun to show in Dostoyevsky's writings, but, of course, the traditional Christian symbolism and vocabulary still prevailed. The new language is contained in the mysterious "laws" of the Samizdat, which I have mentioned, laws which our contemporaries understand right away. Why, from their cribs people are used to perceiving their world and themselves entangled in a web of countless "laws of nature." One could not disentangle oneself from them, but one could put them to use by "subjecting oneself" to their powers and by being aware of them. No matter what, these laws allegedly continue to determine man's destiny completely, whatever his desires and the aspirations of his soul may be. And then all of a sudden appear some new "laws," linking the deepest aspirations of man's soul with the outside world (religio in Latin means "link"); and strangely enough, the laws of the outside world begin to make the most important thing a man yearns for come true, often without his even realizing it. When man strives for a goal and believes in it, then that goal, in turn, moves toward him just as in the proverb, "the prey follows the best hunter." It follows him according to some unknown "laws," and not by accident or some traditional command of God. Thus, something that is considered to be an accident becomes a "law," and the "law" is more understandable to our contemporaries than God. The new language makes a man aware that there exists a definite connection between man's inner world, his faith, his hope, and his love on one hand, and the outside world on the other hand. Then that inner world influences the life of the world in a "rightful" way. To express that idea in the language of the New Testament: "You will be rewarded according to your faith."

But it is not a matter of just translating the old language into the modern one (this is why all the efforts of the Catholic Church to update the *Book of Revelation* remain futile), but a matter of experiencing for oneself the eternal mysterious truths of the old book. But what a hard way to comprehend these "laws"!

QUESTION: If the most important thing is that a person realizes his immortality, his uniqueness, and his dependency on the nonhistorical center, how and what is one supposed to build in history, where everything repeats itself and is final and depends on historical centers?

ANSWER: But dear Mr. Pomerantzev, that is just the problem: The fall of man began when he believed that everything in history depended on historical centers and not on the nonhistorical center. And I do not like that word you used—"to build." It brings to mind either a Tower of Babylon or Stalin's forced construction works. Everything that man builds is so inferior in comparison to what is already created in nature that I can't help doubting the truth of the theologians of recent times (and especially the Catholic ones after Teilhard de Chardin) who saw the scientific-technical taming of nature as the "cooperation of man and God" (Imitatio Dei) and not as the devil's business. In the Bible it is often said that the most important thing is to concentrate on the nonhistorical center, which is in us, and the rest will take care of itself. Of course, you could argue that this very nonhistorical center insists on some historical actions and constructions. Well then, one has to follow that inner inclination, even if nobody in history ever took that road, or even if that path required one to sacrifice not only oneself but a beloved son. There is a "law" which will stop the hand from raising a knife just in time, that is, if the hand is raised not from wickedness but from faith as great as that of Abraham. And vice versa; if, for instance a poor but gifted student, crushed by external, insoluble circumstances, and not believing in any historical centers and their power on heaven or earth, attempts to solve scientifically the problem of bringing full benefit and even salvation to many young and good people by liquidating the mean old moneylender (Dostoyevsky's *Crime and Punishment*), then an unknown "law" will be *helping* him in his murder. That is a link between the inner and outer worlds. It is not "base, and superstructure" straight or upside down, it is not psychocosmic parallelism, it is something that we still do not have any name for, but what the Samizdat writers call "laws."

Is there then a criterion which would prove to a man that he is indeed following the nonhistorical center and going the right way and not following some mirage in his dazzled eyes? Yes, there is. The elder Zosima (again in the work of Dostoyevsky) states it when he says that "men are created for happiness and those who are completely happy are really worthy of saying to themselves: 'I have fulfilled God's precept on this earth.' All the just men, all the saints and martyrs were happy."

Have you ever seen a happy fascist or a happy KGB man? The difference is like that between the enjoyment of a sadistic maniac and genuine love.

Novi Sad, April 1973

NOTES

1. N. Mandelstam, *Second Book of Memoirs*, p. 187.
2. Ibid., p. 205.
3. Ibid., p. 539.
4. Ibid., p. 73.

The Absurdity Of Nonideology

The term "nonideology" has appeared more and more often recently, mainly due to the attempt at rapprochement by the ruling cliques of the USSR and U.S.A. It is alleged to be a necessary condition for a "detotalitarianization" of the Communist world. "Nonideology" is persistently supported by numerous American sociologists and liberal scholars, and by the academician Sakharov in Russia and Djilas in Yugoslavia. The last even proclaims that an era of disintegration of all ideologies in the world has arrived and that this fact should be acclaimed, because the human race needs no ideologies whatsoever.

The official Soviet party theoreticians, on the contrary, regard the concept of nonideology as a screen for a completely defined ideology aimed against the "dictatorship of the proletariat" and consequently say it should be fought against as a variety of "ideological diversion."

In my opinion the Soviet party theoreticians are right in defining it, and the very idea of nonideology only confuses and complicates the realization that the Communist totalitarianism will remain essentially invulnerable until the time when a new all-embracing post-Communist ideology of antitotalitarianism matures and crystalizes.

It is an irrefutable fact that at present all the dominant ideologies are disintegrating; but to conclude from that fact that no ideology is needed is either to manifest superficiality in thinking or to refuse consciously to see the intense ideological search most strongly expressed in the Soviet Samizdat. Although Sakharov's request to "abolish the ideological obsession" in the USSR is quite understandable, it does not at all mean that every ideology leads toward obsession and that an evil and false ideology can be fought only by rejection of any ideology, as Djilas recommends, for instance.

In the encyclopedic sense, ideology is a definite, all-embracing system of ideas in one's social consciousness (it used to be called more precisely "Weltanschauung"—world view). Thus we can talk about Marxist ideology, the ideology of the classical liberalism which permits ideological pluralism, solidarism, existentialism, structuralism, national-socialism, Zionism, socialism. We also can talk about the ideology of Catholicism, and even of Freud's psychoanalysis because of its attempt to give a total explanation of human life.

However, the profound meaning of the concept of ideology is not in a system of definite ideas but in the very existence of man's consciousness about life, the cosmos, and himself, the consciousness that he only tries to express by the system of ideas—Weltanschauung. And without this consciousness about himself and the world man cannot live on earth. In this sense when Sakharov and Djilas come out against ideology it is as a result of a completely defined consciousness, and that means, in the end, of an unrealized ideology. (Similarly, the refusal to participate in the Soviet "elections," explained as a lack of interest in politics, is precisely a political act which breaks the system of active unfreedom.)

In the conditions of active unfreedom, "nonideology" is justified as the first (and only the first) step on the road to spiritual liberation from the bonds of false ideology, a step which is sometimes provoked exclusively by tactical consider-ations. In the democratic world, however, there is no justifica-tion whatsoever for the supporters of "nonideology." Unwit-tingly, they are opening the door to the Marxist ideology, which so successfully advances in the West thanks to its all-embracing "explanation" of all phenomena and all life.

It is possible to fight false ideology only with genuine ideol-ogy, and not with the "nonideology" that leads logically and empirically toward the refusal to comprehend the world at all, thus giving support to a false consciousness. Putting it metaphorically, the enemy army can be made weak by wide-scale desertion, but the decisive victory is won only by the fighting of your own army.

In our time the most urgent need of the human race is not to solve the problem of war or peace, or the problem of the lack of food and energy, or even the ecological problem. Its most vital need is a new consciousness, i.e., a new, all-embracing, profound ideology which would bring order to that unbelievable chaos in human minds which is virtually the basic difference between contemporary man and men of all other eras. The minds of our contemporaries are a complete mishmash of cybernetics, telepathy, genetics, anthroposophy, different religions, Marxism, Freudianism, flying saucers, and an endless number of facts, notions, and systems of thought, sometimes mutually exclusive. (Not to mention propaganda and all kinds of scientific discoveries which increase daily.) But just as from a hundred rabbits one cannot make one horse, thus from the ever increasing number of facts and ideas one cannot create an ideology. Evidently what is needed here is that extreme degree of spiritual tension which melts all the mixed parts of the present consciousness into one ingot, a tension which hardly depends only on the human will.

The failure to understand this, and the propagation of "nonideology," are witness to the incredible lowering of the level of the human spirit and thinking. And that lowering was provoked in the East by the long-lasting totalitarian dogmatism of false ideology, and in the West by the practical materialism which has led some supporters of "nonideology" to such idiocy as to claim that the pseudospirituality of totalitarianism can be fought against successfully only by the material goods of the "consumer society." Sartre was really right when he wrote in his "Criticism of Dialectical Reason" that "the most outstanding characteristic of our time is the fact that history progresses without knowing anything about itself."

Unfortunately, it often happens that even many intelligent and well-meaning men do not understand the tragedy of the fact that our world has no new all-encompassing antitotalitarian ideology. Like the former American ambassador in Moscow, the late Charles Bohlen, they believe that everything would be hunky-dory if "the Soviet Union would start acting as a country and not as a party." Never again will any country in the world be able to "act as a country." All the mistakes and failures in the international policy of the most powerful democratic country in the world, the U.S.A., are the direct result of the attempt to still "act as a country," to use Mr. Bohlen's words. We are witnessing right now a violently growing *planetarization* of mankind. There are no longer any internal or external issues which would concern only a single country. The double-standard of ideological, moral, and other values against which Solzhenitsyn raised his voice with such strength represents exactly that tragic absence of planetary consciousness.

A question inevitably arises in the mind: Are the polemics among the enemies of totalitarianism on ideological issues needed, are they indeed allowable? Do they not weaken the already sparse number of people who are coming out openly against one-party dictatorship? Was Solzhenitsyn supposed to conceal that he was not in agreement with the ideological positions of Sakharov, although he completely supported the academician politically and morally? Should I have abstained from criticizing "the theory of the convergence of two systems" of Sakharov (*New York Times,* July 26, 1971) and "the theory of alienation" of Djilas (*Survey* 2/83, Spring, 1972)?

I am of the opinion that if anything at the present moment is absolutely necessary it is an utterly open polemics that does not slur over or hush up anything. It alone can create, after half a century of forced silence, the ideological preconditions for a spiritual rebirth.

Besides, such an open polemics would help supporters of "nonideology" to avoid in the end playing the comical role of Moliere's Monsieur Jourdain, who was flabbergasted when he found out that all his life he had spoken in prose.

1973

Some Timely Thoughts

(Concerning Letter to the Soviet Leaders by A. Solzhenitsyn)

> "Authoritarianism is a principle of the anti-Christ"
> —Nikolay Berdyaev, *Russian Idea*[1]

It seems it is the way life is destined to be: no barrel of honey is without a spoonful of tar. Thus, simultaneously with *Gulag Archipelago* was published Solzhenitsyn's *Letter to the Soviet Leaders*.

Well, one is now justified in saying that *Gulag* has the same meaning for communism as the records of the Nuremberg trial have for national-socialism. For undoubtedly, just as no one until the end of history will be able to separate Hitler's movement for the "new Europe" and the Nazi swastika from the horrors of the Nuremberg Annals, no one will ever be able to separate *Gulag Archipelago* from the Communist movement. *Gulag* is going to be alive and topical as long as there exists in the world even the slightest worship of Lenin, "dictatorship of the proletariat," October Revolution, the red star with the hammer and sickle. Eternal glory to the author! Just as after the Nuremberg trials, after *Gulag* the world will never be the same.

This is precisely why it is so difficult to talk about *Letter to the Soviet Leaders*. One would like so much to pass over it in silence and simply pretend that it does not exist, never did and never will exist.

But a Russian proverb says: Not even an ax can cut down what is written with a pen. Solzhenitsyn's *Letter* does exist, it will exist, and unfortunately one cannot brush it aside. I would have never written this essay, if after reading the scores of both critical and eulogistic articles, written by Soviet dissenters, Western authors, old and new Russian emigrés, I could have found, along with a lot of useful and intelligent observations expressed, that which is most important about the *Letter*. No, I would have never undertaken to write this essay, because I understand what a great responsibility I am assuming when I come out at this very moment against the social and political program of the creator of *Gulag*.

But, to repeat the words of Solzhenitsyn himself, to keep silent and do nothing is an even greater responsibility.

A great writer is always a *witness*, even when he describes people and events that he has created in his imagination and that do not exist in reality. This holds true even more in the case of Solzhenitsyn and his *Gulag*. Yes, Dostoyevsky's Raskolnikov, Tolstoy's Pierre Bezukhov and Anna Karenina, Solzhenitsyn's Ivan Denisovich did feel, think, and act exactly in the way described and not in any other way. The spirit of genius of a writer consists in the very truthfulness to life of his testimony. Extremely rare, however, in the history of mankind are the *witnesses* who can make sense of their own testimony to a great extent, let alone to take upon themselves the role of ideologists and reformers of society. Tolstoy the writer is one thing, and Tolstoy the preacher of "plain and simple living," and "nonresistance to evil," and the founder of "Tolstoyism" is quite another. The author of *Crime and Punishment* is by no means identical to the Dostoyevsky writing as a political publicist in his "Diary of a Writer," prophesying that in the near future "Constantinople will be ours." I mean the author is the same, but in the first instance he recreates the deepest reality of the human soul and therefore often becomes a prophet, and in the second instance he attempts to "think" on the sociopolitical level and to show the way to the people. But these are two different affairs, two different spiritual spheres.

There is nothing new at all in what I am saying right now. All this people have known for a long time. What is new is only the fact that in our time, which is aspiring toward an integrated, total interpretation of the world (the very aspiration which gave birth to the pseudototality of totalitarianism), there are no more internal affairs on our planet. Or maybe it would be better to say there are no more "external" affairs, because all that is happening is our *inner* business. Besides, the separation of human activity into different spheres, the main inner and the external spheres, is not endurable. Thus the reader, and especially the reader in totalitarian countries, has a very hard time differentiating between the writer-witness and the writer as social reformer.

Gulag is a huge book and *Letter* is a short one. And since there is not much time, the *Letter* is going to be read more widely than *Gulag,* and the author is going to be judged on its merits.

This is why it is necessary to separate Solzhenitsyn the writer from Solzhenitsyn the ideologist of the Russian national rebirth. To differentiate between *Gulag* and the *Letter* and to protect Solzhenitsyn the artist from Solzhenitsyn the social reformer is the most vital thing. It is all the more necessary and urgent, because everything the writer bears witness to in *Gulag* contradicts what he preaches in the *Letter.*

Solzhenitsyn is dear to me (I have written a good deal about him since 1962, first in the Yugoslav press and then in the world press), but the truth is dearer to me than Solzhenitsyn. And the truth, as I see it, is in danger in that, under a certain set of circumstances, the spiritual harm of his *Letter* could exceed the benefit of *Gulag.* Solzhenitsyn is verily The Great Witness, but it was not his destiny to comprehend the meaning of his own experience.

Many just criticisms were expressed about the *Letter* from all points of view: humane-progressive (the article by the academician Sakharov), scientific, democratic, ecological, economic, political, technological, philosophical, etc., etc. But, perhaps because Solzhenitsyn openly laid special emphasis on the rebirth of Christianity, the deeply *anti-Christian* spiritual line of his *Letter* remained totally unnoticed. And this anti-Christian structure of his message in the *Letter* concerns not only some of his various positions, but almost all of his views on the important aspects of the social life. And since Russian culture has always been, from Pushkin to Bardyaev, Christian-Universal, and not narrowly nationalistic, in the spiritual sense, then, the *Letter* by Solzhenitsyn can be judged also as *anti-Russian*.

The Soviet leaders are naturally not going to accept voluntarily Solzhenitsyn's program, because they are not at all motivated by the forces and aspirations that Solzhenitsyn ascribes to them. However, at the moment of the upcoming inevitable crisis of the Soviet system, which is going to come about either by a clash with China, or as a result of the intensification of the internal opposition, or even by conflicts among the "leadership," the program expounded in the *Letter* (excluding its democratic elements) will become *unfortunately too real and possible.* Only on such an ideological platform could Russian slavery be prolonged and, most important, justified for many, many more years. Hence, the *Letter* represents a tremendous danger and a trap for the future of Russia and mankind.

POWER AND IDEOLOGY

The *Letter* could be thematically divided into three parts: first, description of the deplorable conditions of Russia and the whole world; second, the analysis of the reason for such a lamentable state (in the author's opinion the culprit in the USSR is Marxist ideology, and in the West, the belief in progress and permissive democracy); and third, the solution to the problem as the author sees it, and that would be the repudiation of "progressive ideology" and the limitless technical progress. It is not mere coincidence that Vladimir Osipov, the editor of the nationalist Samizdat paper, *Veche* (Vetche was the popular assembly in ancient Russia—Trans.) called *Letter* "the manifesto of the century." Indeed, the *Communist Manifesto* consists also of the same three parts.

The descriptive part of the *Letter*—"Testimonial"—is unquestionably the best part and also the least vulnerable to critical analysis. About ten years ago I also had to write about the dangers of a future war with China, about the backbreaking slavery of women in Soviet society, about the impasse humankind was led into by faith in the endless scientific-technical-progress, and about almost everything else Solzhenitsyn discusses. And I was not the only one who discussed these issues.

But the *central* part, the analysis, in which throughout the *Letter* the author is proving that everything is the fault of the Marxist-Leninist ideology is untenable. In that part, *everything is wrong*, from the first word to the last.

According to Solzhenitsyn, the leaders of the Soviet state have from the very beginning been faithful servants of and even slaves to a false ideology (and an unscientific one at that), and hence all the misfortunes and the misery. Therefore, he sees the answer to the problem as rejecting the false ideology and starting to serve the genuine national interests of the Russian people.

It is puzzling that Solzhenitsyn the thinker did not notice what Solzhenitsyn the writer told us in his books. It is improbable that there exists in the world or even in history men more free of serving *any ideology* than the Communist leaders. And this is not something that happened today; it was like this from the very beginning, from Lenin himself. It was Lenin who demonstrated how one can freely manipulate the Marxist ideology *in order to grab power*. He was the one who turned Marxism upside down in creating the theory of the "weakest link of capitalism" existing in the underdeveloped countries. Marx stated quite the opposite. Not the Bolsheviks, but rather the Mensheviks served the ideology, because for the Bolsheviks from the very first day until the present time, the ultimate goal and the basic motivation has always been the thirst for power, and power alone. For them, power is an end in itself. And their ideology did not determine anything, but was just the means which, always depending on the necessities of power, was sometimes rejected and sometimes changed beyond recognition. With Lenin at one time the slogan was, "The state and the revolution" and it was to abolish any statehood; then came the total reverse: with Stalin it was the "withering away of the state through its reinforcement." Thus, absolutely all of the examples cited by Solzhenitsyn in an attempt to demonstrate that the ideology is to blame for everything, tell us *quite the opposite*.

It was not the ideology which destroyed the Soviets in 1918, but the introduction of the one-party system, which by the way, did not exist with Marx. No "adherence to the evil Western doctrines" is to blame for the forcible collectivization of the peasantry and the destruction of small trade. The writings of Marx (and even Lenin) do not contain such doctrines. Ideological reasons were not behind the great purges, the formation of the prison-camps, and the trials of people by the special triumvirates. Solzhenitsyn himself demonstrated magnificently in his *Gulag* that the ideological reasons did not have anything to do with it. The invariable aim of the long bloodshedding terror was always the same: consolidation of the boundless power and destruction of even potential enemies (of the power and not of the ideology). The only hero who is genuinely ideologically obsessed that we can find in

Solzhenitsyn's opus is the prisoner Rubin from *The First Circle,* the most honest of men.

The struggle waged in the Soviet Union against religion is not for ideological reasons, but for power. For a religious man always deep in his soul remains *free* of the party or any other earthly power. The dissenters are not put in psycho-prisons because the ideology is unable to refute their critical statements, but because they are *expressing themselves* without being asked to do so. When General Grigorenko was put in prison, he was a Marxist-Leninist and he served the ideology, and not those who imprisoned him.

Through all of its history, the USSR has never led one ideological war, and the foreign policy of the Kremlin was never determined by ideology. (Yes, it was often justified by ideology, but that is something else.) Let's consider this: the pact with Hitler, the extradition of the German-Jewish Communists to the Gestapo in 1939-40, the liquidation of the Comintern during the war, the betrayal of the Spanish Republicans in the civil war (done to set Hitler on the Western democracies since there was a fear that the victory over Franco would rally them), the liquidation of the Greek Communist movement of General Markos after the war. Many, many things of that nature reveal that the Marxist ideology did not have any influence whatsoever on the foreign policy of the USSR, from the time when *social-democratic* Georgia was annexed under Lenin.

In both Hungary and Czechoslovakia the Soviet troops intervened least of all for ideological reasons, because both Imre Nagy and Dubcek were Marxists. There is no better proof that Stalin's politics were never determined by ideology than his conflict with Tito in 1948. At the moment of the clash, and for some years after it, ideologically Tito *was no different from Stalin in any way.* The problem was that due to the independent Yugoslav partisan movement, Tito was not Stalin's puppet and therefore depended less *on his power*, which, as it is known, "the wisest of men" could not stand.

For years Stalin was supporting, not Mao Tse-tung, as Solzhenitsyn maintains due to his wrong ideological postulates, but on the contrary, he supported Chiang Kai-shek; and Mao began his "great campaign" and the civil war *against* the demands of the Comintern. And only when it became clear that Mao and not Chiang Kai-shek would win in China did Stalin change his stand. Whether Mao has nursed a grudge against Moscow since then, or whether he has forgiven the "genius" is unknown. However, it is beyond doubt that even Mao is not a slave to ideology, but uses it as freely as Lenin and Stalin did: first it was "the blossoming of a hundred flowers," then "the great leap," and then "the cultural revolution," and now friendship with America.

Alexander Isaievich directed his indignation at the wrong target. Ideology has nothing to do with it. Ideology is not to blame for Russian's becoming a "voiceless appendage" of Moscow. Can Moscow be regarded as "vocal"? Ideology is also not at fault in the destruction of nature and the environment, because in that respect the USSR lags behind the industrial West, and, anyway, is there an ideology one can speak of in the West? As a matter of fact, it is precisely the "New Left" and different Marxist groups that are fighting for the preservation of nature.

If the party needs progressive ideology in order to support or expand its power, then it is used to the hilt. If the ideology begins to stand in the way it is promptly put into mothballs. And from the mothballs is dragged the "old Russian flag, serving as Orthodox gonfalon." Yes, but the flag and the gonfalon did not make it any easier for the labor camps and prisons, a fact to which Solzhenitsyn himself bears witness.

The issue is not at all ideology, or that, in Solzhenitsyn's opinion, the Communist Party leaders in the Soviet Union are aiming at false goals guided by a false ideology. The issue is that they do not follow any ideology, and their one and only goal has been and always will be power. Milovan Djilas described this marvelously in his *The New Class:* "If it [communism] had other aims besides power, it would have to allow for other forces which would then compete with it and lead a legal struggle with it."[2]

If the party's goals were really defined by an ideology, even a "progressive" one (for instance, world revolution, building of socialism or economic growth), the party monopoly would come to an end spontaneously. Let alone if the party had such goals as proposed by Solzhenitsyn. Therefore, the freedom to serve even ideology is already in itself a giant step toward liberation. To serve ideology is *no less* dangerous for the worshipers of power which the Communists are than the negation of ideology. One occurrence, at first glance seemingly paradoxical, is very significant. Namely, in Yugoslavia, during the present attempt to turn toward a total dictatorship, the first to come under attack by the party monopoly were the Marxist professors connected with the journal *Praxis,* who are completely consistent ideologically. They are dangerous by the *very fact* that they serve the ideology and not the party. Stalin did not destroy Trotsky, Bukharin, Zinoviev, et al. for ideological reasons.

The Communist Party leaders of the Soviet Union are not interested in ideology but in *conformity of thought.* Or rather, they are not even interested in whether everybody thinks the way prescribed by the last party plenary session, but only that they *do not think* at all. The ideological lie has been forcibly implanted every day already for decades, not because the leaders have believed in it for a long time. Even now they do not believe in it, and they repeat from inertia whatever they inherited and which is nothing but a "plywood" prop. No, it is forced because every forcibly implanted ideology (not only a "progressive" one) is a tool for spiritual enslavement, and, in that sense, is indeed not only a "plywood" prop.

Evil lies not in the ideology, but in the acceptance of the principle of *authoritarianism* of any ideology, religion, or doctrine.

EVIL OF ANY AUTHORITARIANISM

In *Gulag* Solzhenitsyn constantly compares the horrid reality of the totalitarian Soviet Union with the authoritarian pre-Revolutionary Russia. Often I have done this also, and of course, the comparison does not come out in favor of the USSR. However, people often forget that the good that existed in czarist Russia, especially in the nineteenth century, was frequently the result of the struggle of antiauthoritarian forces of the Russian intelligentsia against the autocracy. In the first book of *Gulag*, Solzhenitsyn writes about it: "The weakening and shaking up the czarist prison system did not come about on its own, of course, but because all society, in concert with the revolutionaries, was shaking it up and ridiculing it in every possible way."[3] But in the *Letter*, we come across a completely opposite statement: "How about the Russian intelligentsia which was also for more than a century devoting all its strength to the struggle with the authoritarian system? What did it achieve, beside enormous losses both for itself and for the common people? Naturally, the opposite of what it wanted."[4] Such a conclusion stems from the wrong ideological position of Solzhenitsyn the social reformer, who wished to prove that all the evil is not in authoritarianism, but in the ideology which justifies the authoritarianism.

With such a point of view one simply overlooks the fact that all the totalitarian regimes of the twentieth century were possible only in the countries with a long authoritarian tradition behind them: Russia, Germany, China, Albania. One can rightfully state that *totalitarianism* is just *extended authoritarianism,* its expansion into all spheres of social life, and the fewer traditions of authoritarianism in a nation the less possibility of the occurrence of totalitarianism. This is proved by the relatively mild Italian fascism, and also "the Prague spring," which was possible only in Czechoslovakia with her democratic traditions. In Cuba Castro replaced the dictatorship of the nontotalitarian type that lasted many years; and, unfortunately, *all the authoritarian* regimes of Spain, Brazil, and Chile, are merely laying the groundwork for totalitarianism. (This is why one feels so frightened for the fate of Portugal—is it going to lapse into totalitarianism or not?)

The February Revolution and the overthrow of the authoritarian system are not to blame for Communist totalitarianism in Russia, but the authoritarianism of Lenin, which found the right soil in the psychosocial traditions of autocracy, which naturally does not mean that the victory of Leninism in Europe would have created a more humane society. Endless streams of blood have been shed, not as the result of the fall of the authoritarian system. They have been shed as the result of, and only after the introduction of, a new, even more authoritarian system, *the ultimate autocratic one.*

So that now, when Solzhenitsyn, with genuine sincerity, comes out and proposes an authoritarian future for Russia, he, in an ideological sense, paradoxically repeats Lenin's sin. Naturally, followers will rush to Solzhenitsyn's side, and they will finish what he refrained from expressing. Already the Samizdat writer Osipov, a nationalist, writes: "To an Englishman, a Frenchman, an intellectual from a capital which absorbed the Western world's outlook, the Russian rejection of democracy seems absurd and disgusting. But this is how a Russian is. While scoffing at the bureaucracy, revolting against dukes and governors, he still loved and respected the czar.... A Russian man needs an integral truth, and he cannot picture it glued together from Social-Christian, Social-Democratic, liberal, Communist, and other truths."[5]

But this is exactly what supported the whole conformity of thought of Stalinism. How long is man going to be flogged?

Solzhenitsyn cries, "Let there be an authoritarian system, but one based not on hatred but on altruism." He writes further: "The authoritarian system does not mean lawlessness and arbitrariness." (As can be seen from his criticism of democracy, he genuinely believes this.) Well, one must repeat something that became an axiom for European juridical thought a long time ago. And that is: legality is the direct opposite of *any* authoritarianism, and it can exist only in a pluralistic, democratic society. Legality is inseparably linked with *the equal rights of all* before the law. Authoritarianism, on the other hand, presupposes unquestionable superiority of one certain ideology, principle, religion, doctrine, and that means of one certain group of people—be it a party, church, aristocracy, scientists—who are then the proponents, carriers, and interpreters of the reigning principle. And it does not matter at all if in that case the issue is Communist, nationalist, autocratic, imperial, or even "Christian" ideology. The problem is authoritarianism itself.

One cannot juxtapose order and freedom, the way Solzhenitsyn does. In an authoritarian system there has never been and never will be order. Order is indivisible with freedom, a fact which the great writer is bound to discover now in Switzerland. Where legislative, executive, and judicial powers are independent from each other, a democratic system exists. In an authoritarian system they cannot be genuinely independent. Is Gogol's famous political pamphlet *Inspector General* already forgotten? Only a democratic system is based on love of mankind.

It has become trite to repeat that it was the Catholic Church's attempt to "Christianize" the world (that should mean love for man!) in an authoritarian way that led straight to the reactions of rationalism and atheism, and also that the activities of the Inquisition and of the Jesuit state in Peru in the nineteenth century are virtually prototypes of the Communist totalitarianism. Their scope, naturally, was smaller, but everything grows and develops, and that means totalitarianism is progressing.

As if he foresaw the appearance of such a "manifesto of the century" as Solzhenitsyn's *Letter*, the Russian religious philosopher Berdyaev, wise with experience and years, wrote before World War Two: "Only those who exposed the social injustice which gave birth to communism have the right to fight communism spiritually. . . . A state which symbolically proclaims itself as being a Christian, theocratic state is the worst, the most harmful for the destiny of Christianity. We Russians have to pray to the Lord that we do not have ever again an 'Orthodox state,' and we have to live by hope that a similar misfortune never happens to us."[6]

CHRISTIANITY AND DEMOCRACY

On the Yugoslav TV screens not long ago, there was shown weekly for two months a new Soviet series entitled "Seventeen Moments of Spring," based on a screenplay by Julian Semyonov. Although the hero of the series was a Soviet secret intelligence officer—a KGB man who worked at the end of the war in the highest echelons of Hitler's Reich—due to the wonderful directing of Tatyana Leonova and the acting of Vyacheslav Tikhonov, the series became a truly artistic creation rather than a stereotyped KGB spoof. The most interesting thing is that the author of the screenplay, Semyonov, crammed into the series a great number of very interesting reflections and thoughts on the totalitarian system. The spectators could not help feeling that those thoughts were about the Soviet Union and that the author was grieving for the fate of Russia. Here is a characteristic scene from the movie: the hero encounters on a train a drunken German general-patriot who criticizes the Nazis and Hitler and who genuinely mourns the destiny of Germany. With tears in his eyes he blames for all the miseries of dictatorship, Gestapo brutalities, military losses ... nothing else but democracy, and he curses it.

At fault for him are not the centuries-long militarism of Prussia, which laid the foundation for a type of unfree man; the German nationalism which was spiritually conceived at the same time with literary Romanticism; the authoritarian system of Wilhelm; or the Red totalitarianism which in turn produced the brown totalitarianism; or the great economic crisis of the capitalist world in the 1930s. No, only democracy is to blame for everything. One feels that the author Semyonov is of the same opinion.

What strange bedfellows these are, blaming democracy for all the ills of this world: an official Soviet writer, the "New Left" in the West, various pro-Chinese groups, Italian neo-Fascists, old Russian emigrés-monarchists, the Samizdat writer Osipov, and with them . . . Solzhenitsyn.

It is true that Solzhenitsyn is cautious and does not openly blame democracy, and he criticizes only its dissolution, believing that Russia is not yet ready for any other system but an authoritarian one. But an altruistic authoritarianism. Nevertheless, one still feels that the democratic society in which every man has the right to have *his truth* and the right to live according to it, does not appeal to Solzhenitsyn, just as it does not appeal to Osipov. For them there is only one truth; how can one allow every man to have some truth of his own?

In order for them not to condemn democracy openly, the following excuse is made: different nations, allegedly due to historical traditions, create different forms of political organization. In the West there is democracy, and in the East we have authoritarianism.

Well, once and for all we have to understand the following fact: different nations do indeed have different forms of authoritarianism and different forms of democracy, but one absolutely cannot equate authoritarianism with democracy under the pretext that they are merely different traditional forms of a nation's political organization of society.

The transition from authoritarianism into democracy means a transition into another, higher sphere of social existence. The most fraudulent, demagogic, bribed election in a provincial American state is, in a moral, ethical, spiritual, and Christian sense, incomparably better than the *entire* centuries-long history of the Russian autocracy (which very often has been heroic, indeed). Just as the pettiest, most cowardly, and worthless man is still on a higher level of existence than the most intelligent brave, and faithful dog. In a man, as in a democratic society, there is ingrained a spark of freedom, which does not exist in an animal and in an authoritarian society.

And while it is true that the will of the majority is not free from mistakes, in an authoritarian state the will of the minority is, in any case, incomparably less free from error. The only difference is that mistakes of the majority in a democracy are always corrected more easily and quickly, and only by such mistakes does a whole society of individual men learn how to think politically in a mature way. On the other hand, the mistakes of the authoritarian minority teach only one thing: the sin of acceptance of any authoritarianism. People cannot be taught democracy by any authoritarian method. The only education is in the active struggle against authoritarianism.

The idea of democracy is not of West European origin, as Solzhenitsyn and Osipov maintain; neither is it of bourgeois origin as the Communists are trying to interpret it. It is of

Christian origin. Unfortunately, in our times this fact is overlooked, even in the West. During the birth of the greatest historical social miracle, which is political democracy, the maternal roots of Christianity were very obvious to people. (Political democracy in ancient times is an altogether different matter, because in the slave-owning society democracy was in reality the oligarchy of free citizens.)

At its dawning John Locke defined democracy on a totally religious basis: a man belongs to God and therefore he can neither give himself up to complete subjugation to another man, nor place another human being under his control; however being "God's property," a man can "entrust the right to administer his will *only temporarily* to another human being who was *freely elected* by him."[7] As a contrast to this, the statement by Osipov that "a Russian does not feel at ease with the uncertainties ingrained in the basis of the electoral system, and also with the calculating and rationalizing of democracy"[8] exudes an obvious idolatry and shows his penchant for the "personality cult."

Democracy's present "revelry" testifies only to its lack, and not its excess. Indeed, "snotty terrorists" appear only where some form of inequality before the law is hidden under the guise of democracy, and that means hidden authoritarianism. They manifest themselves in the form of racial clashes in the U.S.A., national disorders in Northern Ireland, or urban guerrilla warfare in South America with its flagrant economic inequalities.

It is not easy to judge if Russia was so completely unprepared in 1917 for a democratic system. In the only democratic election in Russia's entire history, the overwhelming majority of people did not succumb to the extremist propaganda (the way the German people did in electing the National-Socialists), and they voted for the most sensible and moderate program of the Essers (Social-Revolutionary Party in the Pre-

Revolutionary Russia—Trans.), which was subsequently accepted by Lenin for his demagogic purposes. The unpreparedness of the Russian people was manifested only in the fact that they did not realize immediately the danger of the new authoritarianism, and later on it was already too late to do anything. (The new authoritarianism was hiding behind the noble goals—a new program of land distribution.)

In the civil war the Russian people did not have any choice at all: the White Army did not promise to realize the will of the people as expressed in the free elections. (They thought of getting to the business of a "system of land tenure" only before the very end, while already on the Crimea.)

And what about now? Is Russia even less prepared for democracy than in 1917? Solzhenitsyn maintains that is so. But how about Bukovsky, Sakharov, and other free-thinking people, including Solzhenitsyn himself? One has to assume that they are prepared, are they not? But until the time when the active nucleus of the people becomes the Bukovskys and the Sakharovs, no basic changes will occur, even if the "progressive" ideology is replaced by the Orthodox gonfalon. That is precisely why Solzhenitsyn's espousal of "altruistic authoritarianism" is the greatest trap, because it diverts the people from the only possible means of overcoming totalitarianism, and that means is the radical resistance to every external oppression, every authoritarianism.

Of course, the freedom which was not gained by blood and suffering is easy to lose, and without the spiritual rebirth no political changes will make people free. But the spiritual rebirth, a *Christian* rebirth, is the ascent of a free man, and not of Russian nationalism, the cult of the homeland, fatherland, and one's country. And if Bukovsky and thousands of other Russian heroes were presently waging a struggle not for democracy, but for an authoritarian, nationally conscious Russia, then the people in the West would be justified in saying that the struggle was none of their business.

Fortunately, however, matters stand differently. Truly, in the Soviet Union the struggle is being waged for the most genuine democracy, which has not as yet been realized even in the West. Witness to this struggle is Solzhenitsyn in his books (and by his whole life), although he seems to overlook this in attempting to create a social-political program. The struggle is not only for Russia, but for all people on earth, even the Arabs (Arabs as human beings and not Brezhnev's puppets).

THE TEMPTATION OF NATIONALISM

Although I completely share Solzhenitsyn's opinions that the crisis of the contemporary world is just the crisis of that spirit of superficial rationalism and atheism born in the Renaissance which attained its fullest bloom in the eighteenth century, unfortunately I have to state that even Solzhenitsyn himself did not dispel this crisis and only perpetuates it. The debate between Solzhenitsyn and Sakharov is nothing but a simple repetition of the discussion which began during the European renaissance. (It had a peculiar counterpart in the argument between the Slavophiles and the Westernizers in Russia in the nineteenth century.)

A Christian and a religious man, Solzhenitsyn is fighting for an anti-Christian authoritarian system, while the scientist Sakharov, who signed the atheistic "Humanistic Manifesto No. 2," is voicing his support for a Christian social program. The schism started in the Renaissance continues.

Democracy thus represents a deeply Christian, and not Western European, idea, and it is the projection of Christianity into the social sphere. On the other hand, nationalism is of Western European origin, and it is of a relatively recent date. Before the Renaissance, or more correctly, before the end of the eighteenth century, there were no nationalisms (soul, body, language, and the land of a nation). In both Western and Eastern Europe there were Christians (the Russian word for peasants is "christiane"), there was an intelligentsia with its Latin, and there were states formed not on the basis of nationalities.

The greatness and the universal meaning of Russian culture of the nineteenth century lies in the fact that it continued to thrive on the spirit of Christian universalism, which by that time had already disappeared in Western Europe. (It had also died out in the Russian monarchy, which had degenerated toward the end of the century from an imperial into a national monarchy.) And again the great Russian philosopher Berdyaev, as if he foresaw Solzhenitsyn's *Letter*, wrote:

The Russian consciousness of the nineteenth century was characterized by universalism and an all-embracing humanity, which has been a Russian tradition. Russian communism only reiterated the universalism of the mission of the Russian people, albeit in a distorted, painful, and sick form. Nationalism is not a Russian phenomenon but rather a Western one, and various nationalist ideologies represent a betrayal of the great Russian tradition. That phenomenon is provincial and secondary, it was always more characteristic of Russians of German origin. The nationalist revival of Bolshevism, which can be detected in the ruling, bureaucratic stratum and which gladdened a lot of people who emigrated from Russia, I would consider as the most ominous outcome of the Russian Revolution, as a new form of imperialism. Even in "internationalism" there is more truth, and Russian truth at that: although that truth in this concept is based on a false Weltanschauung. [9]

I believe that the historical role and the token of a great future for America lies in the fact that the United States is not a nationalist state, and God forbid the disaster if Americans change their universal, all-embracing human consciousness by taking on a nationalist one, the way Solzhenitsyn would have it.

If the way out of Communist totalitarianism were indeed a return to an "altruistic authoritarianism," and a "nationally conscious" one at that, then the Samizdat writer Osipov would have been right when he rebutted Sakharov and complemented Solzhenitsyn in expressing the "horror of all the painful futility of our half-century of sufferings."[10] But Solzhenitsyn the witness tells us in the second book of *Gulag* that the sufferings were not futile, and he even blesses the prison and torments he went through, in the process of which he became a "man" (in Christian terminology it ought to be "person"). This means that the torments were not futile, that the totalitarian hell that Russian nations and other nations under Communist rule are going through is not senseless.

And if this is so, then a program of the return to a Russian national-Orthodox authoritarianism can make everything senseless. To quote a prominent Russian thinker, Stepun: "By treating the Bolshevik evil as an absurdity, a destructive tempest which fell upon the righteous Russian life without any reason, we only rob ourselves of the possibility of seriously struggling with it."[11]

There will be people who will ask how one can constantly criticize the relatively mild czarist authoritarianism, in the face of the most horrible totalitarian slavery, and even admit that it has a deep meaning. The plain truth is that totalitarianism, by endlessly augmenting and exposing the ultimate anti-Christian essence of authoritarianism, has threatened to totally destroy the very life of a man. By jeopardizing life—the human soul—it only provokes enormous, desperate forces of resistance in the soul, and thus the miracle of the rebirth of a free man, which is the foundation of a democratic system has its ideology, which is often not realized by people, but it is *not*

102   *Underground Notes*

authoritarian. This is the essence of the issue. The ideology of a democratic society is *determined* by the inner aspiration toward God. All authoritarian ideologies (including that of the church in history) are, as opposed to the democratic ideology *defined* by the striving toward power. For them the end is totally identical with the means. The aim of this power is power itself, and it absolutely cannot be just a means to educate a man in freedom.

In his *Letter* Solzhenitsyn touched also upon the problem of the endless technical-industrial progress which threatens to annihilate all living things on this planet. However, that is a question of the basic goals of our entire culture, and not a political-social, much less an ideological, question. (Ideology is always derivative and is determined by the goals; by itself it determines nothing.) I would say that the issue can be raised only in a democratic society. This problem of the thirst for power over nature and all of life, which is the basis for not only endless technological progress but the very idea of science, related to the thirst for power which is the motivating force in communism. However, the elucidation of the common roots of that drive toward power exceeds the bounds of my criticism of the political-social program of Aleksandr Solzhenitsyn.

Novi Sad, Yugoslavia, 1974

NOTES

1. YMCA Press, Paris 1971, p. 157.
2. Frederick A. Praeger, New York 1961, p. 197.
3. YMCA Press, Paris 1973, p. 461.
4. YMCA Press, Paris 1974, p. 45.

5. Vladimir Osipov, "Five Objections to Sakharov." *Russian Thought,* June 27, 1974, Paris.

6. N.A. Berdyaev, "The Spanish Tragedy before the Judgment of Christian Conscience," *The New City,* no. 14, Paris 1939, p. 24-25.

7. *The New City,* no. 8, 1932, p. 18.

8. Osipov, "Five Objections to Sakharov."

9. N.A. Berdyaev, "On Social Personalism," *The New City,* no. 7, 1933, p. 57-58.

10. Osipov, "Five Objections to Sakharov."

11. F. Stepun, "On Freedom," *The New City,* no. 13, 1938, p. 38.

Djilas versus Marx:
The Theory of Alienation

In May 1971 Milovan Djilas published an article in *Encounter* which in the Serbo-Croat original bears the title "Alienation as Humanism" (Otudjenje kao ljudskost), and which is directed against Karl Marx's Theory of Alienation. Bearing in mind that Stalin and Stalinism can be criticized quite openly in Yugoslavia but that it is unfortunately still not possible to express one's opinions about Lenin or Marx freely, nor to point out that Stalinism is not a deviation from Leninism and Marxism, but rather the logical outcome of Marxist teaching, and remembering also that Djilas is still not allowed to publish in his own country, it is obvious that to enter into polemics with him is a very delicate business. It is impossible for political reasons to criticize or to comment on his books and articles inside Yugoslavia, whereas any criticism from the democratic world could well be made use of by Yugoslav officialdom in order to undermine Djilas's reputation among Yugoslavs at home by means of the argument: "You see, they don't think much of Djilas in the West either."

I believe that because of a coincidence of circumstances I am perhaps the one person at the present time who can polemicize with Djilas on an equal footing without the implication of any political unpleasantness. Some years ago I openly came out in favor of Djilas in my articles, and, like him, I am denied the right to publish in my own country.

Djilas's achievements in his exposure and his analysis of Communist totalitarianism can never be valued too highly and his *The New Class* will undoubtedly remain one of the fundamental works about communism and Stalinism. But whereas in *The New Class* Djilas still in many respects remains a

Communist and a Marxist, i.e., that new society in whose creation he had himself actively participated is criticized from a Marxist position at the center of which is to be found the ideal of "the perfect society," of equality, and of complete classlessness, in his second theoretical book, *The Unperfect Society*, he sets out to criticize the very idea of the classless society. And in his article "Alienation as Humanism" he seeks to strike a blow right at the heart of Marxism, at Marx's Theory of Alienation.

This time the blow is not aimed at Stalinism, or even against Leninism, but against all the contemporary currents of neo-Marxism and in particular against the New Left, in which Djilas rightly sees the ideological vestiges of unexhausted totalitarianism.

Criticism of Marxism can be advanced from several points of view. It can be demonstrated that the "alienation" of man is not conditioned by exclusively social factors so that the changing of these factors alone cannot solve the social problem; it is possible to show that the abolition of private ownership does not at all do away with the division of labor, nor with the class system itself; it is possible to dispute the idea that it is the class struggle which has set in motion the whole process of human development; it can be denied that the introduction of the "dictatorship of the proletariat" leads to the withering away of the state and towards the establishment of the kingdom of freedom etc., etc.

However, Djilas's originality lies not so much in his refutation of Marx for the way in which he advocates the liberation of man and the elimination of human "alienation," as in his assertion that "alienation" is in no way evil and even that it is nothing less than humanism. In other words, Djilas does not criticize Marxism from one of the usual standpoints, viz: that the very manner by which the "kingdom on earth" is brought into being leads not to freedom but to enslavement; that the realization of the classless society and of communism is quite simply not possible; that the realization of the classless society and of communism is eminently possible, but that such a society would bear no relation to human freedom and would mean the spiritual and later the physical death of humanity, and hence the search for a means of creating a bearable way of life should be carried on in a completely different direction.

No, Djilas's point of departure for his criticism of the realization of the "earthly paradise" is not one of these three basic propositions. With his characteristic determination and courage he starts off with the statement that no alienation of man exists and that what Marx and all other Marxists since have considered evil and qualified as "alienation" is in fact something extremely good and represents nothing more nor less than humanism, and that, because of this, no liberation of "earthly paradise" is needed.

It is this basic idea which obliges me to appear in the strange role of the defender of Marx against Djilas, with whom I am otherwise in the main in agreement, and this is all the stranger since I am not a Marxist; but I hope to prove that Djilas, even though apparently such a radical opponent of some of the basic ideas of Marxism, is nevertheless still a Marxist, even in his criticism. In other words, I, who am not a Marxist, will try to defend something in Marx which I consider correct and which Djilas attacks from a position, which I, in line with Marx's own reasoning, consider incorrect. I believe that it is highly instructive to analyze Djilas's original idea, because that idea provides an excellent illustration that it is impossible to criticize Marx by remaining on the same spiritual plane of European rationalism from which Marx himself evolved.

Although the Theory of Alienation, as Djilas correctly indicates, is the least clear section of Marx's teaching, it nevertheless contains the basic starting point, or perhaps even the fundamental motivating principle of the whole Communist doctrine, and the concept of "alienation" is implicitly present in the works of Lenin, Stalin, and Mao Tse-tung despite the fact that they do not explicitly mention it. Stated simply it is as follows: the world is ailing (the Theory of Alienation), it must be cured (the Theory and Practice of Communism). As I have already pointed out, criticisms of Marxism are usually made up of refusals to accept the diagnosis of the ailment (i.e., its cause), or the manner of its treatment. Djilas claims that no ailment exists so that treatment is unnecessary. The premise is highly original, but in order not to fall into an exclusively terminological error, it is as well to compare briefly what Marx understood by "alienation" and what Djilas understands by the term.

It must be clearly stated at once that for Marx the essence of human alienation was the absence of freedom, the enslavement of man, which he saw in the main in the social system of private ownership and commodity production. There is no need to enter into an analysis of Marx's concept of "commodity fetishism," etc., since such analyses illustrate only what Marx sees as the reasons for man's lack of freedom; for Marx the least free man of all was the capitalist hired worker. It is important that Marx sees alienation both in the result and in the act of production. He writes: "Labor is external to the worker, i.e., it does not belong to his essential being; . . . in his work, therefore, he does not affirm himself but denies himself . . .does not develop freely his physical and mental energy but mortifies his body and ruins his mind. The worker therefore only feels himself outside the work, and in his work feels outside himself. . . . His labor is therefore not voluntary, but coerced; it is *forced labor*. . . ."[1] Without going into the question of Marx's theories on the causes of man's lack of freedom—coercion, forced labor, etc.—this is what is of prime importance. And this absence of freedom renders free development of the creative forces impossible for the majority of mankind. It is with this meaning and this meaning only that Marx uses the

Underground Notes

concept of alienation; so indeed in the Marxian sense it could be said that the German or Soviet forced labor camps, in which man's freedom was reduced to a minimum, were harsh examples of the alienation of man. Djilas correctly points out that for Marx alienation is just another expression for the exploitation of labor, and that the symptoms of alienation in an individual, alienated, unfree man show a close similarity to the symptoms of medical neurosis. Marx is correct in stating that the greater the degree of nonfreedom to which man is exposed, the more frequent does the appearance of true clinical neurosis become. The important thing, here, however, is to reemphasize that for Marx "alienation" is identical with absence of freedom.

What, then, is "alienation" according to Djilas? "There can be no doubt whatever," he writes, "that man when he discovers a truth, or when he creates a work of art, or when he improves a skill, puts into his creations, i.e., 'alienates' to them, his power, his feeling, his intellect. . . . Man is man insofar as by his actions he moves away—'alienates' himself—from the conditions of life which nature has given him. . . . Therefore, it is not because this or that method of production (his social condition) has this or that characteristic, that man 'alienates' himself from it, but because (and because only then) he cannot exist in such circumstances any longer. The process of alienation is a way of human existence. The ever greater division of labor does increase alienation, and it makes it more complex; but this does not alter the fact that even primitive man alienated himself in the very act of 'starting' to think, and act, differently from animals. . . ."

And Djilas elaborates his concept of "alienation" further:

Every time that man, by whatever action, achieves something fundamentally or radically new, he alienates himself. It must be that he estranges himself from the conditions and circumstances in which he has hitherto lived. In other words, whenever he creates, and insofar as he creates, he alienates himself. . . . In reality, geniuses create new forms by moving away from the forms they have found. . . . For such an alienation to come about, more is needed than talent: an inner, intellectual and emotive effort which no outside obstacle, social or material, is able to stop. . . . Every human action which creates something new is, at the same time, an alienation from the old, from the existing. . . . Alienation from nature is obvious as a long-term process, and is nothing else but man altering, through technical and other improvements, the circumstances of his existence. . . . In the process of such alienation, man does not stop being what he is, but becomes more independent, more alienated from nature. Man becomes man by alienating himself. . . . There is no end to this alienation from nature, and to that "purely" spiritual alienation, in the same way as there is no end to the universe of which we are part, and in which we exist. . . . The change, the alienation of which I speak here, is personal and free. . . . The human being thus manifests himself to us as creative, hence infinite in his creativeness and existence. Alienated, creative man is one of the aspects of mankind . . . he aspires to complete alienation—the absolute dominion over nature. For it is only an aspiration, part of the ceaseless movement into new circumstances and new possibilities.

It is quite understandable that Djilas at the height of his eulogy to "alienation" should exclaim: " 'I alienate myself' means: 'I am man.' "

It seems unnecessary to go into Djilas's division of "alienation" into three different kinds: alienation from society, from nature, and from oneself, any further; the more so, since of the third type Djilas himself writes: "to me this is its most mysterious aspect. . . ." Nevertheless, something else is quite clear, and that is that the "alienation" which Djilas so exhalts has nothing whatsoever to do with the alienation which Marx speaks of. I even believe Marx could have signed his name under Djilas's text on "alienation" with a clear conscience, given one small terminological alteration, that the term "alienation" as Djilas uses it be replaced by the more usual terms for the manifestations he describes, namely: progress, creativity, evolution, revolution; or stated as briefly and precisely as possible: *what Djilas calls "alienation," Marx called "praxis."* Djilas's description of "alienation" is an excellent illustration of Marx's thesis on Feuerbach which concerns the "change of the existing." Djilas's criticism of Marx is evidently criticism only in appearance. Djilas's "alienation" changes towards better, more human conditions of life, of the state of existence; for Marx, alienation is the state of existence which must be changed, as Djilas would say, "alienated." The contradiction is only apparent and, quite the reverse of wanting to strike a blow at Marxism, Djilas's work on "alienation" remains well within the framework of Marxist thought. It is sufficient to change the terms and there is then no real difference between Marx and Djilas. Marx says that the world has to be changed, Djilas says it must be "alienated," but what they both understand by these terms is virtually the same thing.

It is strange that Djilas has not noticed that he is repeating in detail what Hegel and Marx say about "alienation," except that they call the process "the elimination of alienation." Djilas himself writes that for Hegel "progressive cognizance, which is apprehension of the world, is the overcoming of alienation," but for Djilas "alienation . . . is nothing else but man altering, through technical and other improvements, the circumstances of his existence . . . alienation, i.e., the improvement of technique and of production . . . alienated and creative man aspires to complete alienation—the absolute dominion over nature. . . ." Whereas for Marx the aim of the Communist movement is the creation of a society in which "unalienated man may freely develop all his powers," that is, create; for Djilas "alienated man is creative man."

It is even stranger when Djilas writes that "there is no alienation in the sense intended by Marx," since "alienation is a state of man while exploitation is a social relationship" and they are therefore not identical. However, for Marx also, alienation is only a result of exploitation, that is, a condition brought about by social relationship. So even Djilas himself cannot avoid using the concept of alienation in Marx's rather than in his own sense; he writes of the neo-Marxists: "Is not the contemporary flight into the theory of alienation itself a symptom of alienation from reality and from one's own reason? Is it not, again, tantamount to the handing over of one's being to other forces?" In the same way and completely in the spirit of classical Marxism Djilas writes that "The industrial revolution which signified an unprecedented scientific takeoff . . . was accompanied by intense exploitation and unbridled brutality over workers and peasants," whereas he reproaches the "socialist" societies that they have not set man free. From this the reasonable conclusion would be that so-called socialism does not free, but not that freedom is not necessary, as it is possible to understand Djilas, if we do not become bogged down, that is, in the terminological complexities brought upon us by the unusual use and definition of the concept of "alienation."

This, therefore, is what Djilas writes: "The alienation of man in nature (Hegel) or in God (Feuerbach) is resolved by Marx by the proposition that the real world must be changed." This is what Djilas believes too, except that for "changed" he substitutes "alienated." In this fashion we might expect praise of all revolutions, including the Communist one, as examples of "alienation" (according to Djilas); so the question which immediately comes to mind is—what exactly is Djilas striving for, is not his praise of "alienation" simply an expression of his spiritual short-sightedness?

But in fact this is not the case, and we can only regret that Djilas did not keep to Marx's sense of the term "alienation," in which case his ideas would have been much clearer and our argument made easier.

The substance of the real, rather than the purely terminological conflict with Marx, comes to light in its entirety in one of Djilas's statements: "Man cannot return to his own essence, for he has never departed from it." This is the basic conflict.

Although the whole Marxist perspective is rooted in history, and is projected in it, there is also to be found within it a religious-metaphysical kernel which both motivates it, and constantly comes into contradiction with the Marxist (and indeed not only the Marxist) idea of historical progress. This is what gives rise to all the other inconsistencies: "the kingdom of freedom" is brought into being by means of dictatorship, technical development leads, supposedly, to the elimination of the division of labor, etc., etc. This motivating, and at the same time religious-metaphysical innermost core of Marxism is given its most explicit expression in Marx's theory of alienation. Djilas quite correctly observes that the concept of "alienation" (in Marx's sense) is of a concealed religious nature. He could well have quoted the Apostle Paul, who speaks of the alienation and enslavement not only of man, but of every living thing subject to the "law of mortality" and which "groans in torment, awaiting its deliverer." And if, in purely religious terms, man is alienated from God, that is, from freedom, and subject to natural laws rather than master over them, as was the case according to the "Great Myth" at the moment of creation, then according to Marx, who did not believe in the "Great Myth" any more, man is alienated from his "generic being" in which he supposedly ought to be free, and will return to his generic being in the future "kingdom of freedom," which is materializing in history.

So according to both the Bible and to Marx, man is alienated from freedom. This is where mankind's ailment lies, and the Bible and Marx differ only in their view of the causes of this ailment and the method of treating it. However, neither the Bible's nor Marx's basic essence of man, freedom, is an historical category, and whereas the Bible consistently refrains from erecting the "kingdom of freedom" within the framework of history, Marx, who believes only in history and rejects all aspects of transcendentality, places the "kingdom of freedom" inside the historical perspectives of this world. But if we were to remain consistently within the framework of the ideal of historical progress as Marx would have wished, then we should be obliged to assert in agreement with Djilas: "Man cannot return to his own essence, for he has never departed from it"; if this is so, then alienation can only take place from the existing state and there thus exists a more comprehensible psychological reason for Djilas's change of the concept of alienation. At the beginning of history there was no freedom, either in the Biblical or in the Marxian sense of the word, but historical progress, especially scientific-technical progress, leads man with every step nearer to an ever freer life; such development has no limits—as everyone knows and as Djilas mentions, the crew of Apollo walked on the Moon! From the point of view of historical development we might well conclude that Djilas is a more consistent Marxist than Marx.

It is unfortunate only, that the idea of historical progress demands an answer to the question of what direction that progress will take, and of the possibilities of man's influencing that direction. According to Djilas it would seem that progress, or as he calls it "alienation," automatically leads to the greater humanizing of man, mastery over nature, etc., "because man is—man." In this way historical progress is only the natural development of man, just as is, for example, a plant's growth. To the question: what should man do if he finds himself in the shoes of a hired worker at the time of the initial accumulation of capital, or those of an inmate of a Soviet camp, or of an American negro or even of a man who is dying of an incurable disease or who has been crippled in a road accident?—Djilas answers: "First and foremost, no man who is mentally sound feels himself alienated [in Marx's sense—M. M.] because nature is different from him or because he cannot understand the process of the production of his own hands: he simply feels inadequately taught or unjustly rewarded." As we can see, this is avoiding the issue, since either the historical life of man is based upon certain laws which he cannot in any way influence—Djilas would not agree with this; we have only to recall his praise of "alienation" as the freely created product of human genius—or progress depends on man, and in that case the basic question concerns the end and direction towards which progress is moving.

But if the possibility of choosing the end and direction of historical development exists, this means that man is only partially dependent on the laws of nature, i.e., that he carries within himself a fragment of something which is not to be found in the rest of nature, and which in that sense is un-natural, or supra-natural, and that is—freedom, free will. If Marx had not been blinded by the "scientistic" ideas of the nineteenth century, he would have rejected the historico-economic determinism of social development, and proclaimed that although historical progress does not lead to communism, it is possible to create the "kingdom of freedom" by fighting for it, just as in practice was happening. But in that case, Marx would have had to acknowledge the effective dualism of man, for no free will, what religion calls spirit, is to be found in the historico-natural world, whereas all of Marx's efforts were directed towards containing human thought within the framework of natural history. For Djilas this problem does not arise, since he moves effortlessly on an exclusively historical plane: "Does any creative religious thinker in our age proceed from the traditional aprioristic dichotomy of man?" Nevertheless this dichotomy is that other dimension which separates man from exclusively empirico-historical reality, and which remains outside the perception both of Djilas, and of his ideological opponent Herbert Marcuse, who in spite of his "revolutionariness" remains a man of one dimension, i.e., the historical one. The reason why Marx completely rejected the dichotomy of man, and Lenin foamed at the mouth with rage at the slightest mention of "religious mysticism," was that in order to achieve the end in which they believed, they had to convince people that alienation, i.e., lack of freedom, was caused by exclusively historico-social conditions, and that it would be eliminated by a radical change in those conditions. Let us see in what religious terms Marx describes the "kingdom of freedom": "Communism . . . is the true resolution of the conflict between man and nature, between man and man . . . between freedom and need, between individual and race. It is the solution of the enigma of history and it knows itself to be that solution."[2] If Marx had not lived in the nineteenth century he would undoubtedly have written in the Communist Manifesto, that everyone who perished on the barricades in the struggle for communism, would have eternal life in the future "kingdom of freedom." But what of this life when the "kingdom" is historical? Those thinkers who negate the absolute are compelled to absolutize the relative. The absolutization of history and demonstrable proof of socio-economic determinism which rules out freedom of choice over the future were necessary for Marx to be able to attract people towards his choice of the future, for it is quite clear that the tragedy of human life on earth does not exclusively consist of a socio-economic system which enslaves, nor can this itself be solved by social revolutions. Djilas is quite correct in pointing this out, and particularly so when he attacks Marx's statement that the root of alienation is in the division of labor; it is evident that a high degree of technological development merely accentuates the division of labor.

But Djilas is not correct when he says that "no man who is mentally sound feels alienated, only . . . inadequately taught and unjustly rewarded." The world is still ailing and unfree even if we accept that one manifestation of the ailment is the appearance of totalitarianism of the Communist type, against which Djilas's intellectual efforts are directed.

One of the arguments against Marxism which seems of particular importance to Djilas is the claim that Marxism is not scientific or rather that the point of departure for Marx's prognosis does not agree with scientifically established facts.

Moreover, historical development has shown that the working class does not get poorer as a result of the pressures of capitalism but in fact richer; the socialist revolution has been victorious in backward rather than, as Marx held, in the most advanced countries; that the abolition of private ownership brought into being a new party-bureaucratic class, and did not establish the foundations of a classless society, etc., etc.

All this is absolutely correct, and all these are arguments which could indeed be used against Djilas. It is strange that Djilas does not notice that his statement that Marxism is not a science but a faith, and that Marx himself first believed in communism and later sought ways of proving his faith, makes it apparent that we are dealing here with two different realities: faith in the possibility of realizing the "earthly paradise" within the framework of history, and science as a neutral agent which can serve any end. The book *The Unperfect Society* clearly shows that Djilas himself first stopped believing in communism, and only later found "scientific" evidence for no longer believing.

In itself, science says nothing either for or against Communist teaching and, further, science neither gives nor proposes any human ends, but is itself conditioned by already determined ends. From the scientifically established fact that workers are exploited, or that intellectuals do not have freedom of speech, it in no way follows that workers should not be exploited, or that freedom of speech should exist. From the scientific fact that the splitting of the atom releases enormous energy, it in no way follows of its own accord that an atomic bomb should be produced, or should be permanently banned. Science gives an answer to the question of what should be done and in what way, in order to achieve a certain end, but science does not give the end itself, even when scientific knowledge is its own end, for in this case the end is a prerequisite and not a result of science. Science says nothing of the need for a just society, just as medical pathology says nothing of the need for man to be healthy. The need for a just society is a prerequisite of sociology, just as is the need for a healthy body for medicine, even though scientific research in these fields can be carried out with a quite opposite end in view, as recent history has shown.

The basic belief of communism is that "the kingdom of freedom" can be brought into being within the framework of history and socio-economic progress by means of "the midwife of history"—violence. Faced with this fundamental basis of communism any scientific facts whatsoever are irrelevant, or at best of secondary importance. The best example of this is the October Revolution and Lenin, which is exactly what Djilas cites in his attack on the Communist ideal. It is true that Lenin stood all Marx's teaching about "the base conditioning the superstructure" on its head, by his conviction that the Socialist Revolution could be brought about in a country where capitalism was undeveloped, and with a working class whose numbers were so small as to be negligible, and that in fact such countries represented "the weakest links in the chain of capitalism." For Marx the weakest links were those countries where capitalism is most developed and where the proletariat is the most numerous class. Even so, Djilas has every right to state that Lenin is a Marxist. The same applies to Stalin's "socialism in one country." Stalin too is a Marxist and here too Djilas is correct, but would any important change in the picture of Communist dictatorship have been seen if today's avant garde of the "alienated"—colored people, students, etc., had seized the monopoly of power in their own hands, as those of the New Left would have wished, instead of the avant garde of the working class, which today lives too well to start a revolution? I do not think so. But is it then in that case of any importance at all that Marx's prophecies of historical development have not proved to be accurate? The spirit of communism, the building of the "kingdom of freedom" by means of the earthly power of violence is still just as alive as it was in Marx's day, and indeed much more so, and no "scientific facts" can serve as an argument against it. It can even be paradoxically stated that Marxism has always existed, but that it is only in the twentieth century that it has achieved such an unheard-of expansion.

Despite the fact that Marxism is not scientific, faith in science and Marxist faith are as alike as sisters, since both have as their basis the progressive domination of the world and nature, and of human nature adopting the *a priori* standpoint that power gives freedom. Such domination, as we have shown, Djilas calls "alienation." It must be emphasized, however, that faith in science and science itself are not identical.

In my opinion Djilas is right in considering the present-day Marxist or rather neo-Marxist philosophers second-rate thinkers, but it seems to me that his belief that Marx's "doctrine is kept alive mainly because it has evolved into the preservative of bureaucratic socialist structures" is erroneous.

Does the power of the state really support the New Left? Is neo-Marxism really institutionalized? I personally still do not see an all-embracing ideal which could be set against Marxism, not, unfortunately, even in Djilas. The danger of recidivist totalitarianism from the New Left is not to be found in the justified claim that people of our time are "alienated" (in the Marxian sense) and unfree, but rather in the belief that dictatorship and violence can set man free. Any violence directed towards "the better organization of human life" is closely linked with spiritual blindness and the conviction that there exists only a single dimension of life, the historical one. And while we remain in this single dimension, we cannot avoid violence, even though the violence of technocracy, which is scientifically based, has been substituted for the violence of partocracy. But since man is nevertheless, speaking in old-fashioned terms, a bridge between two worlds, the spiritual and the natural, then as a result of the spiritual blindness brought about by the spread of rationalism and belief in science, true aspiration towards the absolute is projected into the historico-social sphere, which is relative to the life of man, and in which only relative freedom is possible; even this is not an immanent historical sphere, but is dependent in its entirety on the extra-historical dimension of the spirit. Freedom is not the result but the cause of the historical process! It is not possible to refute Marx or the New Left by remaining on the same natural-historical plane. It is only possible by spiritually overcoming Marxism, and that means overcoming faith in the historical unidimensionality of life.

Such is the criticism of atheism, a prerequisite of any criticism of modern barbarity—to paraphrase Marx, since the belief is in unidimensionality, in being alienated from the sphere of the spirit, that is, from freedom.

By all accounts, the breakthrough into the other dimensions of life seems to necessitate some spiritual process initiated by a breakdown of the belief in communism, and that without that faith and its breakdown, such a breakthrough is extremely rare. It can be freely stated that in the first decade of this century it was initially made by those Russian thinkers, who at the end of the penultimate decade of the last century had introduced Marxism into Russia, and who participated in the so-called first Marxist front; it was they who had the opportunity of observing the first Russian Revolution of 1905; Berdyaev, Struve, Boulgakov, Frank, and their journal *Vekhi* of 1909 have remained even to the present day the inevitable signposts in all efforts to vanquish Marxist faith in violence. Some distance apart from them, but on the same road, stands the solitary but perhaps greatest of all figures, Lev Shestov.

It is interesting to follow the parallel courses in the process of spiritual emancipation from Marxism taken by Djilas and by another former Marxist, Berdyaev. As early as the end of the third decade of this century, Berdyaev gave a definition and a short characterization, and indeed the very concept of the new class, which Djilas a quarter of a century later was to take as the basis of his well-known book. The same thing was to be repeated with the idea and concept of *The Unperfect Society*, which Nikolai Berdyaev described several decades earlier in his book *The Fate of Man*. I know for a fact that Djilas did not know the Russian philosopher's book. This parallel process gives hope that all those who outgrow the Communist faith in spirit and in life will proceed along the same road.

As distinct from Berdyaev, however, Djilas has not yet reached the final stage of overcoming the unidimensionality of the historical process; this is apparent in the work which we have analyzed.

Yet another former Communist, Ignazio Silone, writes in his latest book[3] that the greatest event in the lives of many people of his generation has been the renewed discovery of Christianity during the last ten years. There can be no doubt that in such cases we are indeed dealing with a revelation, and not with "scientific knowledge," since it is the discovery of another dimension which gives man the strength to oppose the force of the historical violence of any totalitarian system and organization, including that of the historical Church. Because a part of man does not belong to the natural-historical world, it will not die with that part of man which does belong to this world; hence the power of this world is not absolute. And this is not because the immortality of the soul (the deepest "I" in each one of us, the kernel of freedom) depends in any way upon morality or necessity, or anything like that, but only because it exists in reality (if you like, in spite of all morality). If such a reality did not exist, then indeed Lenin and Stalin would be invincible. Fortunately they are not, in spite of the continuous campaign against a recognition of the existence of the life of the spirit.

From all this the following conclusions may be deduced:

1. Djilas's criticism of Marx's theory of alienation is only apparent, because Djilas always remains within the framework of that sphere of thought which created Marxism. Djilas himself writes that man created neither nature nor himself, but he does not grasp that man could not have created the most implausible and unnatural thing that we know in life, that is freedom, freedom of will. He believes that freedom is the product of some human development, he does not see that freedom is a prerequisite of any development, and by this very fact cannot have historical roots. The materialization of freedom, which is always concrete and historical, is quite another matter, but the question of the progress of freedom is a very problematic one. The unceasing struggle for freedom in history must surely show that man was originally created free, and no myths about man's "fall," about his alienation, and finally in its ultimate development—neurosis, could exist at all if freedom were only the result of development. The oppres-

sive weight of unfreedom can only be felt by one who has once been, or is in his heart of hearts, free but has been cast into an unfree state. Franz Kafka expresses it very well: "Who can bemoan a lost kingdom? Only an exiled king."

2. Marx is correct in stating that man is alienated (unfree), but his theory and practice for the elimination of alienation based on historical violence serves only to show that he himself was a deeply alienated man (not of course in Djilas's sense), and that in fact his teaching about liberation is the clearest symptom of his ailment and not a remedy for it. But man is alienated not from some abstract "generic being," but from the real, extrahistorical center of his own personality and from the inner kernel of freedom within himself (speaking in religious terms, this kernel is that man was created in God's image). Alienated, or separated, but we must remember here that the devil—diabolo—is the mythical divider. It is naive and irrational to deny the existence of the ailment, for it does exist, even though Marx was wrong in his diagnosis and therefore in his therapy also. Marx is in many ways reminiscent of a Biblical prophet who answered God's call and was given the commandment: "Go and make the people blind so that they look and do not see, listen and do not hear!" But contemporary history shows that the curse of blindness is still with us.

3. Without the discovery of the reality of the other dimensions of the struggle, no criticism of Marxism from any "scientific" standpoint whatsoever, or victory over totalitarianism, is possible. The theory and practice of Marxism can always be changed, the "weakest links" can at one moment be the developed, at another the undeveloped countries, the bearers of "revolutionary violence" can at one time be proletarians, at another peasants, and still later "coloreds," etc.; but the same spirit of Marxism, the institution of totalitarian dictatorship loses nothing in the change. At its basis is to be found the intermost essence of all totalitarianism, the belief

that power gives freedom. Against this belief in power can only be set the belief that all power enslaves, and enslaves primarily him who wields that power, and that to suffer violence without resistance is just as wrong as to commit it.

In Ignazio Silone's latest book, the hero of the story addresses these words to his adversary, the pope, the representative of the historical earthly kingdom:

> If you cast a glance through the window, on the steps in front of the cathedral you will see an old and ragged beggar woman, someone who in the life of this world means nothing; she sits there from dawn to dark. But in a million years, in a thousand million years her soul will go on existing, because God created it immortal. But the kingdoms of Naples, of France, of England and all other states with their armies and fleets, and all the rest, will thus be turned into nothing.[4]

This says all there is to be said about the "kingdom of freedom" on earth and in history, in history which would not exist at all if there were not something above history which some call God, others freedom, and still others purpose, and which has no connection with the natural laws of development, which are the only concern of science.

Belgrade, 1971

NOTES

1. K. Marx and F. Engels, *Rani Radovi* (Early Works) (Zagreb: Naprijed, 1967), pp. 246-49.
2. K. Marx, Kapital (Capital), vol. 1 (Belgrade: Kultura, 1947), p. 275.
3. Ignazio Silone, *Sudjba Odnogo Bednogo Hristianina* (The Destiny of A Poor Christian) (Rome, 1968).
4. Ibid. p. 264.

Comments on
The Unperfect Society

These comments were written after reading a manuscript of the book in March, 1970, a half-month following my release after three and a half years' imprisonment under strict isolation. Since the comments were not written for the purpose of publication, but essentially for the author of *The Unperfect Society*, the comments as drafted are distinguished by their condensed form and occasional personal appeals to the book's author. Since *The Unperfect Society* has by now been translated into many languages,* and a Russian translation is also expected in the near future (Possev Publishing House), I therefore deemed it useful to publish these comments. At the same time I decided not to revise them, but to leave them in the original, first of all, because I regard my thoughts concerning Djilas's book to be equally correct at present and, secondly, out of fear that in the process of revision the immediacy of my reaction after initial acquaintance with the manuscript of Djilas's book might well disappear.

—Politically superb. Written most opportunely.

—This is a declaration of political position.

—During the next twenty years, future developments will proceed in this direction.

---

* This article was translated by V. N. Pavloff.

Translator's note: The English translation used for all quotations and references, with paging indicated, is: Milovan Djilas, *The Unperfect Society: Beyond the New Class*, translated by Dorian Cooke, London (Methuen & Co., Ltd), 1969. See also the American edition: New York (Harcourt, Brace & World Inc.), 1969.

—Extremely important features: resistance to "neo-Marxism," the search for and indication of the paths for victory over totalitarianism.

—The book is original, even though it does not in itself represent a complete, up-to-date synthesis of personal fate, communism, Yugoslavia, history, etc. . . .

It is superbly stated that:

—The dialectic was made subtle by human reason (page 57), i.e., precisely the view for which Lenin reproached the Machists.

—Marxism, even though it does not recognize this, is the last of the unique scientific systems (page 88).

—The term dialectical and historical materialism is "a slogan absurd as such because the second part of it means only application of the first part to human history, and the first part of it is based on the postulate that each phenomenon is historical" (page 86).

—The abolition of private ownership represents in fact only a change in the form of authority.

—The so-called renascence of Marxism—a new revolution—is absurd since it does not provide any guarantee against a repetition of past occurrences (page 38).

—The simultaneously developing demands for political freedoms in the East and the tendency toward socialization in the West are giving birth to "a world-wide comity of men" (page 117).

—The main hindrance to progress is the party bureaucracy's power monopoly, which through "the ideological economy" inhibits all economic forces and, for this reason, Yugoslavia has become one of the leading exporters of labor (page 129).

—In Yugoslavia the regime found itself obliged to introduce reforms and did this without any ideological motivations whatsoever.

—What is most important today is the expansion of political

freedoms and the economic liberation of nationalized industries as well as of private concerns (page 130).

—The leaven of discontent is working precisely among the disgruntled Communists (page 138-139).

—Capitalism is adapting itself to social needs without major upheavals (page 134).

—In society, stratification is occurring vertically from senior party officials to peasants, rather than horizontally (page 151).

—According to the author, who still uses Marxist terminology, "a special middle class" is being created (page 146); the future belongs to this class and the author is naturally on its side (page 147). Theoretically this is somewhat indefinite, but in political terms it is exactly so.

—It was a very useful bit of information that the Communist Party of Yugoslavia was, on the author's initiative, renamed as the League of Communists (page 155). The same relates to the concept of "self-management" (page 157).

—It is correctly stressed that society without authority is not viable, is a utopia, or a paradise, and that those who maintain that they can live without a political attitude have already in effect submitted to one (page 166).

—Valuable likewise is the author's admission that the realization of the ideas, which he had earlier shared, would actually have led to the most rapid intensification of real social problems rather than to their solution (page 161).

—Extremely important and courageous (taking into account the author's situation) is the thought that "the ordeals of independent-minded people and the repression of youth in the East lie upon the conscience of the New Left in the West" (page 170).

—Every society needs a radical opposition, which would arouse it from time to time (page 168).

—It is possible to struggle successfully against the Communist dictatorship only by nonviolent means (page 182). Berdyaev thinks likewise (and so did Jesus Christ).

—Under normal conditions, Communist dictatorships perish. For their consolidation, they need struggle (page 187). Hitler even said: "If there were no Jews, we would have to invent them"; whereas Orwell in *1984* wrote "the heresy of Goldstein will live forever." Mao Tse-tung follows the same path.

—The author finally and irrevocably rejects violent methods of struggle (page 187).

—Plotters and conspiratorial organizations would neither desire to overthrow nor succeed in overthrowing the Communist dictatorship (page 188).

—Extremely significant and fruitful in its ideological consequences is the thought that "freedom fighters in the Communist world must have no less confidence in their ideas, their role, and their capabilities than the Communists had in their struggle for power" (page 192).

FEATURES WITH WHICH I AM DISSATISFIED:

—Repetitious references, for example, pages 35 and 166, to "the demoniacal" or "the divine," the sweetest of all enjoyments, the enjoyment of power. In human terms this is understandable, but politically such a sincere admission on the part of the author of possessing an incurable thirst for power and glory (page 166) is indeed harmful.

—The terminology is often neither sufficiently clear nor precise, as for example, the demoniacal enjoyment involved in the recantation at the Central Committee Plenum in January 1954 (page 174). "It lacked only the penitent, and I relished the thought that I could fit the bill with my 'recantation' " (page 176). This "enjoyment" is somewhat disturbing.

—Frequent explanations, especially in the beginning of the

book, of basic historical facts or concepts (for example, libido, eschatology, etc . . .). Ten years ago in Yugoslavia this may have been useful; at present this is unnecessary.

IDEOLOGICAL COMMENTS

Djilas writes that the dissolution of the world center of communism into a number of different states proves that communism is not a religion, but a political movement, because while it was an ideology (which Djilas very nearly equates with religion) it had to have a world center (page 145). It is sufficient to mention the Christian religion, which, despite the existence of three major churches and several hundred sects, in its essence remains a religion, so that the author's statement is debatable. Indeed, elsewhere, Djilas compares the contemporary dissolution of the world Communist movement with the Protestant movement in Europe, in which the schism was produced by the opposition of "increasingly powerful princes, rather than in differing interpretations of dogma." Nevertheless, further on, we learn that "Catholicism purged itself as a religion in the Counterreformation" (page 145). All of this involuntarily leads one to believe that the author identifies religion with the Church. However, there exists only one Christian religion, even though there are many churches. Nevertheless, in the book we find the assertion that "the gradual weakening of the Vatican's secular power resulted in an actual strengthening of its role as a religious world center." Consequently, on the one hand, the author asserts that weakening of secular power strengthened the religious significance of the center; whereas, on the other hand, for example on page 10, we read that "international centers . . . were bound to become great powers in their own right."

Even if we allow that many misunderstandings in the book

are due to imprecise terminology, from which the author suffers, it is still impossible not to observe an even greater contradiction on the same page 145; from the author's reasoning on this page one could readily come to the logical conclusion that, with the breakup of the international secular power of one Communist center (Moscow), the ideological role of this same (or another) center must inevitably be strengthened. Nevertheless, the entire book affirms the exact opposite, i.e., the dissolution not only of the movement itself, but also of the ideology.

Concerning nations, in several places Djilas asserts that nations are timeless, that they "survive in the shadow of communism today" (page 132). One may assert this only if he believes in the immortality of the soul—individual and national—in which the author apparently does not believe, since we have no empirical confirmation of the timelessness of nations. Almost all existing nations, as well as their languages, are of relatively recent origin, provided that we do not count the somewhat more ancient Jews. It is sufficient to recall the eternal confusion of philologists caused by the fact that the Normans often accepted the language, faith, and customs of a conquered people, and in this way considerably troubled those historians who with the aid of philology have been trying to solve the riddle of still relatively recent European history. Another example—the Americans. The Americans are a living example of the fact that spiritual freedom is more important for man than ethnic origin. The Americans are largely the descendants of various religious sects of the Old World, who had there been subjected to persecution. The true homeland of man is freedom and, raising an objection to Djilas, we could say that the breakup of the international Communist movement into separate national ones represents merely a return to the original position from a false path, false because the internationalism had been based on such passing and fictitious realities as "class" and so on. At the same time, it is precisely this dissolution which shows that without a supranational spiritual reality it is impossible by means of technology, socialization, and so on, to solve world problems. Despite everything, this dissolution is useful, since the whole issue lay in the choice of a false path.

"There is no equality among nationalities without human freedom, or without the genuine right of each national community to . . . its own armed forces" (page 153). Provided only that it is not a tactical step, this assertion exactly proves the entire absurdity of creating state organisms on the basis of nationalities—if we take into account only the incredible ethnic mixture which exists in Yugoslavia and, incidentally, in the whole world as well. Besides, this assertion is debatable. Let us remember Switzerland.

"Luther believed that the sinless man would have no need of laws" (page 92). Luther merely repeated a basic idea of the Apostle Paul, the first ideologist (Christ was not an ideologist) of the new young religion. This idea is the basis and the essence of all Christianity and ascribing it to Luther is equivalent to asserting that the idea of the destruction of private property belongs to Tito. I think it is necessary to be more cautious with quotations.

"Marxist philosophy . . . has wrought transformations unparalleled in human history" (page 91). This declaration is excessively audacious, if we consider that Marxism as a movement really extended and lived for only one century, and then began irrepressibly to break up. Let us call to mind only Christianity and Islam, which have existed for centuries, and compare the transformations wrought by them with those of Marxism.

According to Djilas, Marx was the first to understand that society, just like any other phenomenon, may be studied. . . .

And how about Auguste Comte? Marx's priority does not lie in this, but in something else.

Einstein and Stalin! The Stalinist view of a complete universe is contrasted with Einstein's endless cosmos! Why was this necessary? Einstein, in particular, with his theories, destroyed nineteenth-century conceptions of an infinite universe. According to Einstein, the universe is *not infinite*. The causes of Stalin's intolerance vis-à-vis the theory of relativity are completely different.

"Every state, every social group, for that matter, always has a natural desire for the status of equality" (page 145). When such statements are made, it is necessary to specify the exact meaning of the concept "status of equality," that is to say, "equality of rights." Let us recall Leo Tolstoy's sneer: "And I wish to be equal of rights with women—I wish to give birth to a child." For Beethoven, equality of rights lies in composing music; for Pericles (and for you, Djilas, as well)—in ruling; for Penelope in being faithful to Odysseus. Unfortunately, "equality of rights" is too often confused with equality. Remember Shigalev in *The Possessed*: "We shall all be equal! We shall tear out the tongue of the genius, we shall cut off the musician's ears. . . . "

"A way of life without any determinable ultimate objective but that of keeping alive . . . " (page 142). I would very much like to know by what method Djilas came to this conviction. Scientific? I think this would be of interest to every reader.

It is superbly stated that the daughter of Stalin resurrected from satanic depths the muffled conscience of her father (page 127). On the same page, the author speaks of persons "who have chosen their own vision rather than the existing realities of life." However, this is already to some extent mysticism. How is conscience inherited—through the genes, or through the spirit? But this shall be discussed later.

It is not necessary to correct Hegel. Djilas writes that "from history, nevertheless, something can be learned about what ought *not* to be done. . . . (page 110). As a matter of fact, the essence of learning is in what not to do, and Djilas's amendments would only refute that statement rather than supplement Hegel's position.

The book gives percentage increases for industrial productivity in the West. But, in the case of the USSR, only the quantity of goods is listed (pages 120-121), so that the reader is obliged to work out his own percentages. However, an even more serious fault is that the author when making his comparisons with prerevolutionary Russia leaves out the period 1890-1917 during which Russian industrial development did not lag behind rates of growth in the other capitalist countries, for which the figures are given. Unfortunately, the author, still blinded by age-old propaganda, obviously does not know the basic facts, especially with respect to the period of industrial progress during the so-called Stolypin reaction. I should be able to supply him with all the relevant data. If Russian industry had continued to develop at the same tempo as between 1890 and 1917, then in 1927 steel and coal production would have already reached the level that the USSR achieved in 1941 on the eve of the Nazi invasion. The author fails to consider the extent to which nonfree labor is irrational and uneconomic in all its aspects. Unfortunately, he occasionally repeats Soviet propaganda.

On page 188, it is stated, that communism had "history's mandate to carry out industrialization." And on page 187, that under communism society moves from the nonindustrial stage to the industrial and postindustrial. However, the facts and also the comparisons with capitalist countries cited by Djilas disprove his above assertions. The same applies to the statement on page 119, that communism hastened industrialization in Russia, China, and Yugoslavia. All, absolutely all, historical experience up to now contradicts this, whereas all the comparisons with capitalist countries are similar to the well-known anecdote: "Say, who before the war was able to acquire a television set?" Today it is already possible to foresee the time when Cuba shall be obliged to import sugar. An edict limiting its use has already been issued. And Russia is importing bread. . . . Djilas is still halfway under the influence of bluffs.

On pages 97, 98, and 102, Djilas maintains that the Communist system serves as proof that it is not the base which determines the superstructure, but the reverse. Meanwhile, on page 133, the author in a completely Marxist spirit asserts that "party monopoly becomes fetters on the mode of production"; on page 31, we read that Marx alone understood that "the entire population of the globe must perforce change and keep changing their ways of life . . . adapting them to improvements in industry"; and, finally, on pages 100-101, Djilas implies that Marx was right because the Communists transformed the world, but "not along the base" since economic forces are invincible. From all this, one may conclude that the impending downfall of communism proves precisely the correctness of Marx's theory insofar as society exists (structure, superstructures) only so long as productive forces may develop within it. This, in essence, is what Djilas maintains throughout the greater part of this volume. It is incompatible with many of the above-cited allegations and incongruous with the description of his own experience in relation to "being" and "consciousness."

Who will, ultimately, destroy communism? "The invincible economic forces" to which people should submit? Or could it be the factor which the author cites on page 141?

"May Marx forgive me one last dereliction: the crisis in communism is not brought about by economic, so-called objective factors, but almost exclusively by human, so-called subjective factors. Strangely enough, these subjective factors are not ideas that grip the masses and so lead to material power. Rather, they are individual acts, a human defiance of coercion, whether that coercion takes the form of brute force or of spiritual domination or, as is most frequently the case, of a mixture of the two. The unfortunate human race, the wretched human being, will endure all evils, even coercion, for as long as it can and must; it will never submit to them."

The above thoughts completely contradict Djilas's entire social and theoretical conception of the downfall of communism at the hands of "the developing base" and confirm his entire life experience and the tribulations through which he has passed: The transformation on the night of 7-8 December 1953 (after which Djilas gradually moved away from official Communist dogmas), which "I . . . was incapable of acting otherwise than I did, even if I had wanted to" (page 20). (Luther made the same pronouncement at the Council of Worms.) The old men in the prison, whose faith was not a "reflection of the real world" (page 24). His self-assertion in his rightness—"not for any rational or scientific reasons, but from purely personal, ideational, and existential reasons" (page 24). His affirmation that "I had not lost my faith" and that this had preserved him. (In essence, this is repeated in all of the Epistles of the Apostle Paul.) The assertion that Marx first became a Communist and only later began to prove his theories (page 81); and, notably, that Marx when working on *Das Kapital* was "establishing 'the absolute truth' of the faith that had been revealed to him in his youth." And finally, Djilas's statement: "The truths that had absorbed my transformed self and were relentlessly devouring it were something I could not reject, even if I had wanted to" (page 126). All of this proves that the essence of man does not depend on any "base" or, more accurately, on any base in the Marxist materialistic conception. Yes, of course, it is not consciousness which determines man and his life. Rather the base is *precisely that force* which brings men into collision with social, natural, rational, intellectual, scientific, mechanized, technical, technological, and cybernetic reality, and this is the timeless part—the human soul. Whenever Djilas speaks about himself, about his own attitude to the world, this can be very clearly seen. However, when he speaks of his social and theoretical realities, his consciousness is still split—Marxist and personal. Nevertheless, this can in no way be described as a shortcoming in the book, since it reflects the spiritual state not only in the socialist countries, but in the world as a whole. Hence the book is very important, essential, and significant, notably in its political aspect.

Djilas, in accordance with his Marxist background, identifies the soul as consciousness. Nevertheless there exist not two, but three spheres: (1) the real external world; (2) the consciousness, which "reflects" in itself both worlds; and (3) the spiritual world, which is no less real than the external. This third world is the one about which the Biblical prophet Job said:

> Oh that my vexation were weighted,
> and all my calamity laid in the balances!
> For then it would be heavier than the sand of the sea.
>
> Job 6:2-3

Likewise, in accordance with his upbringing, the author asserts a number of incredible things—that religion lacks revolutionary social significance (his personal example and his following his internal voice prove the contrary); he equates revelation with a moral way of life (page 26); he says that religions have not contributed any real criticism of communism, "it is just not in their nature to do this" (page 27). However, at the same time, he maintains that in disassociating himself from Marxism, he became more attached to "the imperative of the human conscience" and to his "firm belief in the inseparability of man from the universe, of personal destiny from mankind's destiny" (page 19). (In religious language, this is called the Church.) He writes that he had found a faith and had been "warmed by it and fortified to overcome vicissitudes and hardships far beyond anything my conscience . . . could possibly imagine" (page 20). It is true that Djilas maintains that he believes in the intellect but, unfortunately, he does not specify what he means by this. All of the preceding are ancient words, words which had sounded already in Christ's Sermon on the Mount. And all of the author's "humanism" has its origin in "Love thy neighbor as thyself." However, suddenly, the author equates revelation and science and struggles against God only because he assumes that God is law. The Apostle Paul wrote: "You were bought with a price; do not become slaves of men." (I Cor. 7:23). Does Djilas comprehend this essence of religious faith? Hence the notion when he assumes that Spinoza absolutized God, whereas Marx absolutized matter. It is true that Marx proceeds from Spinoza, but Spinoza equated God with nature (matter), and thereby in the human consciousness of the new age killed the very meaning of God as freedom, freedom even from the laws of nature. When Djilas rebels against Marx, he is, without realizing it, simply repeating the words of Jesus Christ or of the Apostle Paul. Of course, he does not delve deeply into the meaning of a quote taken out of context from Luther (or Paul). This, I repeat, is because of his unfortunate earlier education (and, incidentally, applies to 99 percent of twentieth-century persons). Or, let us say, when the book's author on page 96 compares Marx with the prophets and with "the founders of the great religions," here likewise he reveals that he had not read the Bible with due care, since the God of the Bible is precisely a living being, who forgives, alters decisions (the prophet Jonah), changes the future in response to great and fervent faith (the fate of Job). And, generally speaking, prophets do not reveal the inevitable, but caution against the future (for example, the prophet Jonah).

Christ speaks about the power of the devil over this world, whereas Spinoza equates the material world with God. And from here exactly come forth Marx and his "prophecies," which are based not on the primary reality, but on the secondary reality, the one which directed the life of the author of *The Unperfect Society*. Just from this incomprehension of God arise the author's words: "I reveled in the fiendish notion that, if the existence of God should become incontrovertible, I would rebel against his omniscience and immutable order" (page 24). Also his assertion that the world is full of dogmas, whereas people thirst for life (page 8), where he again confuses revelation and dogma. For, if Djilas truly knew the Gospels, he would remember that when the Apostles inquired about His path, Christ replied: "I am the way, and the truth, and the life" (John 14:6), but He certainly did not postulate any empty dogmas. (He had himself reproached: "Woe to you, scribes and pharisees . . .") Religion is not a dogma, it is not a system, but a *living link* with the depth of existence, with the entire cosmos. However, the depth of existence is not contained in atoms or stellar constellations, but in that other reality which inspired Djilas to withstand the whole world.

On page 185, Djilas expresses his "doubts about the scientific infallibility and universal relevance of Marxist ideology," and on page 184 he maintains that the essence of his conflict with the party lay in his realization that "ideas themselves can never be much more than symbols, recognizable aspirations" and cannot by themselves uplift people. The author also maintains (page 56) that science destroys dialectical schemes.

All of this, of course, is most incongruous with the assertions cited earlier that the author had been fortified by faith and that this had occurred precisely despite his own consciousness.

Out of all the above one can draw but one conclusion, namely that the author had failed to ultimately clarify for himself the question of what constitutes science.

If we consider science in its classical rationalistic-Marxist meaning as the cognition of that which exists, then we fall into a closed circle out of which there is no exit. Cognition of what exists involves in itself the assumption that the consciousness of the cognitive person is located beyond the existing. However, the entire systems of Heidegger and Jaspers are based precisely on the concept of the inseparability of existence from the human consciousness. Most clearly of all, this closed circle displays itself in Lenin's *Materialism and Empiriocriticism*, where Lenin, wishing to remain a consistent materialist, literally maintains that materialism, that is to say, the scientific understanding of the world, occurs solely in the recognition of the existence of a certain objective reality outside our consciousness, which is primary in relation to this consciousness. In this way he wittily attempts to refute Mach and Berkeley and, not without success, shows that the real world existed even before the appearance of human consciousness. Naturally, Lenin does not even notice that he is merely repeating the tradition, in fact Biblical, that the world was created before man; and once again wishing to remain a consistent materialist, he maintains that the human consciousness is nothing other than highly developed physical matter. Thus, in these two theses Lenin in essence asserts the following: matter, i.e., the objective world, is all that which is found beyond human consciousness. And human consciousness is only the highest stage in the development of matter. The contradiction here is quite evident, since in the first assertion matter is everything that is not consciousness, whereas in the other assertion, consciousness itself is essentially matter.

In the greater part of his book, Djilas is still unable to free himself from these Leninist theses (in reality Marxist, only taken to their logical end), despite the fact that his entire life and experience (concerning which he bears witness that he had been supported by faith) speak of the existence of yet another dimension, which in the language of religion is called faith. The Apostle Paul defines faith as a profound inner knowledge of that which it is impossible to perceive by the rational, scientific path. Hence faith is in some manner knowledge, but knowledge of the existence of a different reality, which in religious language is called spiritual reality. This is the reality which the Biblical Job spoke about, the very real reality which compelled Luther and the author of *The Unperfect Society* and, in some ways, Marx and Spinoza as well, to rebel against all of the so-called objective reality. If Djilas had been better acquainted with the writings of Luther and of Saint Paul, then he would have seen to what extent, when speaking of his own experience, he repeats the words with which the same experience was described by Luther and by St. Paul.

Hence, even without examining the issue of to what degree the human consciousness does or does not merge with objective reality, in speaking about science we must first of all solve the question of what we concretely regard to be science. If under the heading of science we imply the knowledge of that which really exists beyond human consciousness, then it is correctly asserted that science destroys all dialectical schemes, as is observed by Djilas on page 56. Meanwhile, Djilas himself, unfortunately, remains under the spell of these same dialectical schemes, since from his book one may yet conclude that science is in essence the realization of the objective world's *law-governed sequences.* Here we already have the addition of one *a priori* and dogmatic assertion that these *law-governed sequences* do in fact exist. Consequently, science as knowledge of the real may also include in itself cognition of a different spiritual reality (which throughout his life governed the author's actions), but in this case we would have to recognize yet another source of cognition besides our senses, namely in religious-mystical terminology, the "oculus spiritualis," the spiritual eye, the inner compass. It is precisely in accordance with this inner compass, which Djilas calls faith, that he oriented his path in life. Incidentally, the same could also be said about Lenin.

In a word, when Djilas says that the world has changed, but that man's consciousness has remained unchanged, this same thought may be applied to the author himself, since Djilas himself does 'not realize which realities guided him in life. Incidentally, this shortcoming is inherent in all of Marxism, since it is the extreme expression of the spirit originating in the Renaissance era.

True science, which also includes in itself cognition about the existence of other realities beyond the empirical, cannot make any *a priori* conclusions about the existence of any laws *either natural or social*. In commencing the investigation of life it is merely able to raise this question. Of course, it is also necessary to include in the investigation the thought that this very approach already predetermines the answers as well. Strictly speaking, the answers are affected by the questions. Contemporary physics itself—not Einstein (as Djilas, unfortunately, asserts) but Heisenberg—indicates to us an exceptionally important and revolutionary fact; the observer, the observation itself, the investigation of nature *alters the object of the observation*. In its far-reaching consequences, this is an extremely significant and revolutionary thesis but, unfortunately, has not as yet brought forth its fruit in contemporary scientific and philosophical thought. Properly speaking, from this Heisenberg thesis there follows a direct path to the religious position, since laws (even including natural laws) exist *only insofar* as man believes in them. Let us recall the words of Jesus Christ:

> For truly, I say to you, if you have faith as a grain of mustard
> seed, you will say this to the mountain, "Move hence to yonder
> place," and it will move; and nothing will be impossible to you.
>
> Matt. 17:20

This far-reaching Heisenberg thesis leads to the same conclusion as the one which Schreider in his own way asserts in the article "Science—the Source of Knowledge and Superstition" (*Novyi Mir*, 1969, no. 10), namely, that the broadening of already familiar *law-governed sequences* in one relatively limited sphere of external realities (since the other reality is not subject to scientific investigation—"the Spirit breathes wherever It wishes") cannot be expanded over the entire reality. Consequently, if we approach reality in the same way as Djilas, "scientifically," *agreeing a priori that in the real world there exist laws*—whether natural laws or social-historical laws— then this indicates nothing other than dogmatism and "scientific superstition." To make the paradox even more striking, the father of modern cybernetics, Norbert Wiener, in his well-known *Introduction into Cybernetics*, published in 1948, himself wrote that if this world obeyed only those *law-governed sequences* which are known to the human mind, then we could expect at every moment that, as in *Alice in Wonderland*, the entire world would before our very eyes be transformed into something completely different, just like, strictly speaking, what would happen in the consciousness of a new butterfly, if it possessed such consciousness. It is Russell, whom Djilas had read, who in a different way from Heisenberg has revealed to the human intelligence the thought that our certainty in tomorrow's sunrise is faith (if it is not superstition) and that the laws which are known to us today may no longer exist tomorrow. Tomorrow terrestial gravitation may suddenly cease. Hence the incorrectness of the entire conception of science as held by Djilas, who praises Marx for having been the first to "scientifically investigate" social phenomena (as we have already observed—Comte was the first). This conception of science is based on an a priori and by no means corroborated faith (if not superstition), from which all of mankind has suffered from approximately the time of the Renaissance and even earlier according to Biblical tradition—from the creation of the world. The statement in the Book of Genesis that "the tree of life" differs from "the tree of knowledge" and that whoever tastes of "the tree of knowledge" becomes mortal and is banished from paradise, translated into modern language, is nothing other than Heisenberg's assertion, carried through to completion, that "the observer alters the observed." Thus, the so-called scientific attitude to the world, *based on the faith* that it is within the power of the observer to change the laws of nature studied by him—this in Biblical language corresponds to "the fruit from the tree of knowledge." Or, again returning to the Bible, when science masters the world, submitting to the so-called laws of nature, science itself falls into the third temptation, with which Satan tempted Christ in the desert:

> Again, the devil took him to a very high mountain, and
> showed him all the kingdoms of the world and the glory
> of them;
> and he said to him, "All these things I will give you,
> if you will fall down and worship me."
>
> Matt. 4:8-9

Science gives power over the world, but also subordinates the living human being to its so-called laws. Technology as the applied form of science utilizes all existence merely as its means. This does not liberate man, but just turns him into a slave. In the language of the Bible: faith in science, reason, consciousness is nothing but faith in Satan, i. e., unfreedom, faith in "the eternal laws of nature." What properly opposes this is not authority over the created world by *submission* to the laws of nature; but authority *over the laws of nature* which, judging by the Bible, had belonged to man in paradise before he had been seduced by "the tree of knowledge." Jesus Christ indeed possessed such power over the laws of nature.

Authority over the laws of nature is the last, the ultimate freedom. According to the Bible, this is simply the affirmation that "man was created in the image of God," man is the son and part of the living God (God is not the God of the dead, but of the living). The authority which science gives over nature (which also in its own way is living), over the animal world, and, as has been shown by Comte and Marx, also over human society—this is extreme slavery. *Such authority requires first of all submission* to the so-called laws of nature and history. And can a slave-driver himself be free? Does the new Adam, Jesus Christ, have need of a motorboat (and science is also necessary here to manufacture it), if He has authority over the laws of nature and walks on the waters? The Resurrection of Christ fulfilled the Glad Tidings that man is free even from the laws of nature, free even over death, as was shown by the Resurrection. The faith that Christ had mastered the laws of nature (as I have already said, the reality of faith and of spirit is really felt only by the "oculus spiritualis") was that force which caused thousands and millions of Christians to go voluntarily to death by martyrdom in the first centuries of Christianity rather than submit to the external real world and its laws. It was in following this same force that many centuries later, the Russian revolutionaries went to jail, to hard labor, and to martyrs' deaths. Still later, the Yugoslav revolutionaries, including Djilas, would do the same—but, unfortunately, just like all the revolutionaries of the modern era, he did not realize this. In short: God exists, but He was on the side of Lenin.

The absurdity of Lenin's thesis, according to which knowledge in essence is nothing more than the possibility of utilizing the real world (Lenin in his book *Materialism and Empiriocriticism* gives an example, I believe it is coal), is not worth debating. Man has since ancient times often utilized chicken, for example, and has even killed for his needs (e.g., fried chicken) many of these living creatures. However, it would be ludicrous to claim that by this means man has been able even to a small extent to unravel the mystery of life and death.

In a word, Djilas possesses a typical split consciousness and, in essence, continues to remain in the channel of that stream whose penultimate representative was Marxism, and whose last representative is "pure science," which the author defends with might and main.

The author does not even raise the question of the existence of God, i.e., of that conscious force which has authority not over nature but over the laws of nature, altering them at His own discretion, and which directly influences the fate not only of mankind, but of each individual person. The author knows in advance that such a force does not exist, that there exist the so-called laws of nature, which are indifferent to persons and to mankind. Nevertheless, this force exists, whether we wish it or not, just as the sun exists and gives warmth and light also to the blind who are unable to see it with their empirical organ of sight—their eyes. The path to such knowledge is opened precisely by modern physics, in part by Heisenberg.

The author, brought up on Marx and Feuerbach, understands God in a Catholic sense—which is characteristic of the West European cultural tradition—as eternal order and law. This concept was taken to its extreme by Spinoza, who, all the same, crowned the efforts of the medieval scholastics. Nevertheless, the scholastics and Saint Thomas Aquinas, who proceeded from Aristotle, as well as Spinoza and Marx and the admirers of so-called pure science, such as Djilas—are all because of the above concept completely in opposition to the living God of the Bible, the Father, rather than the master of man; and likewise in opposition to absolute freedom, freedom from the laws of nature. Hence, Djilas does not understand the basic argument of the Apostle Paul that law came in order to kill man, that "where there is no law, there is no crime" and, finally, that Christ freed man precisely from laws (eternal and imminent), i.e., from death.

If there is no God—i.e., a force which has power over the laws of nature—then there is no freedom, because in the empirical world, in which the laws of nature rule, there is no freedom. And if man is not part of the divine being, then he is the slave of the so-called objective world and its laws. However, the entire life of the author and the personal experience described by him speak against this.

Because of the contemporary, unfortunately in large part Catholic and Protestant, spiritual climate in which Marx and Engels and Feuerbach grew and developed, Djilas constantly identifies God with law. However, the truth is the contrary: God is the rejection of all law, God is absolute freedom, and man is free insofar as he is the son of God. And on the contrary, he falls under the power—in Biblical language—of Satan, when he is subjugated to law. And the primary faith in laws (laws of the development of nature, matter, history, human society, etc . . .) is the foundation and basis of modern "pure science," which the author defends but which, in essence, is nothing other than the extreme extent and the last stage in the development of the same spirit that produced Marxism, against which the author, as it were, rebels. For this reason, I am stressing the constant conflict between the author's personal experience and his consciousness.

Djilas also often confuses religion with the Church, and this is not by chance. Under religion he incorrectly implies a social historical organization of people. The very word "religion" means "bond." Religious dogma is that which may, in Marxist language, be called "the reflection" of this bond between the deepest essence of man, that part of the human personality which is free from the real world and which we call "the soul," and the all-encompassing essence of life—God. "Fortified by faith" simply means, without any guarantees and knowledge given to us by the external world, to follow this inner imperative—in religious language, "the voice of God." Here Lenin (and Marx) are right, that consciousness does not determine man's being, but the other way around. As the penultimate stage in the completion of the modern age's tradition, as the base, they take the so-called objective real world, over which with the aid of knowledge and submission to law-governed sequences, man is able to rule. However, the essence of man—that part of him which is independent of the objective world, the part of God in man—is human freedom.

When we approach the world "scientifically," that is, when we look for the laws which dominate the world, we simultaneously recognize not only the existence of such laws, but also the independence of these laws from our will and thus from the will of the living, conscious, omnipotent God. (Otherwise, why would we have to comprehend such laws if we could change them in accordance with our will?) Luther, whose words Djilas uses continually (without realizing that they are Luther's words) describes that inner spiritual imperative which forced him—despite his own consciousness and the entire historical reality—to stand up against the whole world and against forces far more powerful than himself, and between ruin and submission to choose defiance. To the horror of all of Catholic Europe (the ancestors of the modern "scientific" mankind)—he cried out: *"Sic volo, sic jubeo, sit pro ratione voluntas!"* (I thus wish, I thus command, may my will be above reason!) Of course, *reason* is nothing other than *the power of law* even in the human soul. The power of the devil. And hence, the Apostle Paul says that we Christians are mad in the eyes of men and wise in the eyes of God. And Christ says that the wisdom of man is madness in the eyes of God.

On page 35, Djilas rightly asserts that power is the essence of all Communist systems, "that, with the passing of time, nationalism has imposed itself as the surest way for Communists to enjoy the fruits of power—that greatest of all delights." Power over nature by means of submission to the so-called laws of nature cannot exist without simultaneous power over man. For this reason, contemporary scientific progress has led to the spiritual enslavement of man and mankind. The Communist movement, to which Djilas used to belong, is an extreme expression of this spirit in the social-historical sphere.

On page 106, Djilas writes that freedom today means "the liberation of science and technology from the strait jacket placed on them by systems of ownership and the like, no less than the liberation of human minds and bodies from dogma and tyranny." Marcuse, nevertheless, is somewhat closer to truth, since he understands that *technology* itself is one of the main causes of contemporary slavery. It is true that he does not go to the end and for this reason does not find any solution. Djilas in this respect is even somewhat behind Marcuse, since his "liberation of science and technology" is in fact extreme slavery. This touches upon the new epoch as extremes which come together; thus one could say that the author of *The Unperfect Society* and the writer of these comments are "brothers-opponents."

On page 109, Djilas pokes fun at the former Marxist Peter Struve, who wrote that the October Revolution was "a great misfortune" and "a big mistake." Djilas, by contrast, says that all that has occurred is irreversible and unchangeable. He has thus shown that he has been unable to free himself from the Marxist dogmas concerning the indisputability and the immutability of the course of history. First of all, the fact that something has occurred and can in no way be changed does not contradict the assertion that the event was "a misfortune and a mistake." This is known to every person on the basis of his own experience. Only if one defends the indisputability of what is happening can one write that insofar as events are irreversible and unchangeable, they cannot be a mistake and a misfortune. Incidentally, religious consciousness affirms that not only the future may change depending on the will of God and the passion of man, but also the past. A Biblical example of this is in the fate of Job, who regained his wife, his children, and his flocks. Among modern thinkers Kierkegaard and Shestov share this view. Iev Shestov wrote: "The truth that Socrates was imprisoned is not eternal, and possibly one day, in accordance with the will of God, the fate of Socrates may be altered." However, I shall not dwell on this, since this realm of the spirit is too far from Djilas.

True to his above-mentioned belief in the immutability of historical events, the author assumes that no one can accuse communism of being no better than other regimes (pages 137-38). First of all, the author himself constantly criticizes communism for this. Secondly, from this point of view one could say that neither fascism nor Maoism can be reproached for anything.

On page 117, the author says that the capitalist system was in essence born and gathered strength only in the West, and that it is only there that socialism can replace capitalism in precisely the way conceived by Marx, namely by the proletariat forcing the socialization of the means of production. This is absolutely true and is already taking place, although not so much under the influence of the base as under the influence of the spirit of freedom, which in the West is still somewhat stronger than in the East. According to Marx, the weakest link in the capitalist system is exactly where the forces of production are most developed. At the same time, Djilas, who, unfortunately, still remains under the influence of Marx and Lenin, criticizes Peter Struve. The issue is that Lenin's assertion to the effect that the weakest link in the capitalist system should be sought in the more backward countries, where the forces of production are least developed, is in complete contradiction with the assertion of Marx. In this respect Lenin, of course, was not a Marxist, but his practice itself completely contradicted the Marxist theory concerning the full dependence of the social superstructure on the base structure. Hence Leninist voluntarism is closer to Luther, closer to the existential experience of Djilas and, in fact, is closer to the Bible than it is to Marx's "historical irrevocabilities." And, for this reason, Djilas's criticism of Struve is illogical and contradictory.

In my opinion, Djilas should not have briefly (and incidentally, quite erroneously) touched upon the major issues of existence in such a way, as though he were at some meeting. For example, on page 180 he writes: "And who knows, if there were no evil inside us, whether we should be the beings that we are. Should we then be able, should we then know how to drive the creative, the godlike powers within ourselves?" Before writing about such things, he should have acquainted himself with the well-known historical polemics on the problem of evil in man, which were debated by Pelagius and Saint Augustine, by Luther and Erasmus of Rotterdam. Otherwise, a rather bad impression remains.

Unfortunately, Djilas is not acquainted with the great Christian philosophical tradition, nor with its direct heirs—the Russian philosophers of the first half of this century. As a result of historical circumstances and of his own unfortunate upbringing, Djilas is acquainted only with the Russian imitators of Western European thought—Chernyshevsky, Plekhanov, Bukharin, and so on. Hence, in his book he involuntarily draws nearer to such shallow Western philosophers as Garaudy, McLuhan, Servan-Schreiber, and even Marcuse. The issue is that the creation of electronic brain bears witness that the human mind is not the basic essence of man—the brain may be replaced by cybernetic machines. This shows exactly that the human mind, the brain, is not man, but only his weapon. This opens the path to the understanding of man's deepest essence which, in religious terminology, is "the human soul."

On page 166, Djilas expresses the thought that "the fight for ideas of any kind is at the same time a fight for some definite form of power and domination over others." And once again he touches upon the deepest philosophical heritage of mankind. From his assertion it inevitably follows that all those fighting for freedom, including Christ, Gandhi, and so on, are, in essence, aspiring for power. If he had carefully read the Gospels, he would have noted how the Jewish elders in a frightened manner speak about Christ: "Who is He who speaks as one who has authority?" However, as may be seen from all of the above, the power of Christ is *of a completely different nature* than the power of the natural laws, than social-political power, than power over living and dead matter, and so on. The power of Christ, the new Adam, i.e., of man as the unblemished son of God who has not yet tasted "the fruits of knowledge," had not submitted to the devil by accepting the irrevocability of the laws of the nature—is power over the laws of nature itself. In accordance with this, social-political power, the power of science, and so on, is the direct denial of the power of Christ. As a paradox one could say that any coercion (and there can be no social-political power without coercion, while scientific technology is, in essence, coercion over nature) i.e., any *such power* is actually *the absence of power* given to man by God. All science, all engineering, all our powerful technology are only improvements in the wheelchair for a paralyzed man. Man, who was healthy before the Fall, had no need of the crutch of science and technology. However, the casting away of the crutch, of course, cannot by itself heal the paralysis.

I repeat that, from the political viewpoint, the book is excellent and very necessary since it reflects the contemporary spirit in more than just our country, Yugoslavia. The often repeated assertion, especially on page 189, that the world today needs not a revolution but reforms, is quite correct. But recall the well-known aphorism of the spiritual heir of the Great French Revolution, the so-called obscurantist Joseph de Maistre: "Counterrevolution is not the contrary of Revolution, but it is Revolution backwards." If we remember that Djilas follows this same thought, this enables his critics from the left and the New Left positions to attack him. Unfortunately, Djilas, despite his very correct political declaration, still does not move away sufficiently from all of these various leftist positions—hence, he is not in a position to rightly defend himself.

Basically, Djilas's book simply reflects to an extreme degree the spiritual prejudice and unresolved contradictions of our epoch. In the case of Djilas, as well as all of modern mankind, the contradictions will be resolved and a new path will be opened in the very moment when, instead of seeing the way out of the situation in the invention of an electronic brain, they *existentially and keenly feel* and with their deepest essence understand the thought of one of the leading "ideologists" of early Christianity, Tertullian:

"We have crucified the Son of God; and we are not ashamed of this because it is disreputable; even dead He rose again—and this is beyond doubt because it is impossible; and I believe in this because it is senseless." (Credo quid absurdum.)

Novi Sad, Yugoslavia
March 1970

A New Approach to
Anna Karenina

> What would become of an axe in space? Quelle ideé. If it were far enough away, it would begin, I think, to revolve round the earth without knowing why, like a satellite. The astronomers would calculate the rising and the setting of the axe, Gatzuk would put it in his almanac, that's all.
>
> The devil to Ivan Karamazov, *Brothers Karamazov*
> by F. M. Dostoyevsky

I.

In 1877, in Russia, a beautiful woman by the name of Anna Karenina threw herself under the wheels of a railroad train.

Her creator, the eyewitness Tolstoy, did not inform us whether she felt physical pain in this last moment of her life, for he was more concerned with the mental suffering from which she escaped into death.

Opinions about the causes of Anna's tragedy have differed for almost a century. Tolstoy himself thought that Anna was to blame in breaking up a "holy marriage," and that the Lord punished her with that kind of awful suffering from which people flee only to death or insanity because of her rotten liberalism. In the last moment Anna turns to her tormentor:

> "No, I won't let you torture me," she thought, addressing her warning not to him, not to herself, but to the power that made her suffer, and she walked along the platform past the station buildings. *

---

*Quotations from *Anna Karenina* are from the Penguin edition, Baltimore: Penguin Books, Inc., 1954.

Tolstoy selected the following verse from the Bible to appear at the start of his novel: "Vengeance is mine, and I will repay." He also had lucidly remarked that an artist is an artist because he describes things as they are, not the way he wants them to be. And once more: "The artist is like the biblical Valat who, wishing to curse, offers a blessing." Since *Anna Karenina* is indisputably the work of a great artist, everything Tolstoy puts down happened just the way it appears in the novel and not otherwise. There is nothing unbelievable about anything that Anna Karenina, Vronsky, Levin or Kitty think, feel, and do. Yes, and Anna dies one death and no other. Let's recall Bergson's remark: "Only great artists who reject abstract concepts can truly depict man's inner life." Leo Tolstoy is a great artist.

But *how* it happened is one thing, *why* it happened quite another. As an eyewitness, Tolstoy is not competent to answer the question why. Therefore it need surprise no one that an artist of Tolstoy's stature gives so unintelligent an answer. In the same way we may overlook with an ironic smile the naive epilogue to his great work *War and Peace*.

It is clear to us, as children of the twentieth century, conditioned to thinking sociologically, that it was the very society in which Anna lived that was responsible for her tragedy, the tragedy of a lively and extraordinary woman.

An article by M. Yuzhin in the *Soviet Encyclopedia* (1946 edition) includes the following: "Tolstoy depicted in that novel, [*Anna Karenina*] the dissolution of a marriage, the breakup of a family, the tragedy of an extraordinary woman who is trying to get away from the deadly embrace of high society and its morals. A beautiful, strong, and human person resists false social laws and, unable to win the struggle, perishes."

In the same encyclopedia (1956 edition) the famous Soviet literary historian N. Gudzy says: "With amazing skill and immense psychological insight Tolstoy presented the tragedy of a young woman who was fighting for her happiness and perished thanks to the false and merciless morals of high society. The range and depth of Anna's feelings, the sincerity, integrity, and humanity of her nature are opposed in the novel to the egotism of Karenin and his circle and the pettiness of Vronsky's character."

West European encyclopedias label Anna "a victim of passion" and offer analyses not essentially different from the Soviet ones. But if society had held love and passion to be normal and natural and central to any relationship between a man and a woman, no tragedy would have resulted.

Thomas Mann has written: "What I have boldly called the greatest society novel in all literature is an antisociety novel."[1] Said Lunacharsky: "We rebel against a god who says 'Vengeance is mine.' We say to every Karenina, be she a member of our class or just a woman, you are entitled to happiness, strive toward light and liberty, be not afraid, you will not fall under any wheels."[2]

We can agree on one thing: society is guilty for Anna's death, not she herself. Everybody would also agree that Anna's suffering from which she escaped into death is a direct consequence of her finding sufficient strength not to give in to social norms, not to act like others and, through her own determination and actions, to smash falsely conditioned social norms. When Anna is punished, society is guilty, for she is innocent. All this points to a historic stage of social development in which an individual struggling for happiness, although innocent, must come inevitably to a tragic end.

Thus, a conclusion states itself: If we create a society in which love and passion are held as the only criterion for a natural relationship between men and women, no other innocent Annas need meet a tragic end.

Such reasoning seems, at first glance, completely correct

and logical. However, some great thinkers forced us to follow Descarte's "De omnibus dubitandum," and doubt such a clear and simple scheme which explains Anna Karenina. But many people throughout history have not agreed that "external circumstances" (social forces, historical stages of development, etc.) are to blame for the tragedies of individuals. Dostoyevsky has said, in *The Idiot:* "You are guilty before all because you could have been a light in darkness but were not," and in his *Diary of a Writer:* "It is about time that we cease to blame society for everything." This has been echoed by Gorky, reminding us of Anna's words:

> "What can I want? All I want is that you should not desert me as you are thinking of doing," she said, understanding all that he had left unsaid. "No, I don't want that . . . that is of secondary importance. I want your love, and it has gone. So it is all over."

and by Nietzsche: "No man has the right to be unhappy"; and by Lev Shestov: "There are no unhappy people; all unhappy people are pigs and they themselves know that best."

It is just when we doubt the truth of any sociologically-based common explanation for Anna's death that Tolstoy's novel confronts us with a reality we had not noticed before: *Anna Karenina* refutes all sociological explanations.

The purpose of this essay is to defend, through a content analysis of the novel, the following contentions:

1. Anna Karenina herself is to be blamed for her tragedy, and not the society in which she lives.

2. Anna was punished not because she acted differently from other women in her circle, not because she broke "the norm and the law," but because, in a crucial moment of her life, she acted exactly as others would have acted.

3. All recent opinions about Anna's demise as set forth in

modern encyclopedias are completely false. They are to be attributed to sociological ideas and theories swallowed whole and, however paradoxical it may seem, Leo Tolstoy came closer to the truth even though he was mistaken about Anna's guilt and punished her himself.

4. Anna's tragedy would, in a more perfect and progressive society, be not diminished but magnified for, then, Anna alone would be responsible for her guilt, including that lesser part of it which can be laid upon her environment in the novel.

The reader is probably already familiar with the story. A young, vivacious, beautiful woman, married to a man whom she dislikes, whose son she bears, meets a man with whom she falls passionately in love. She finds enough strength to leave her husband and live with the man she loves in the face of society's general censure. But tormented by her separation from her son ("crucified on a cross of passion and maternity") and deeply wounded by the disdain and contempt shown her by society, she chooses suicide.

> And the candle by which she had been reading the book filled with trouble and deceit, sorrow and evil, flared up with a brighter light, illuminating for her everything that before had been enshrouded in darkness, flickered, grew dim and went out for ever. (p. 802)

Racked with unbearable accusation and pain, she goes to her death. Her pain is her punishment for having broken the law. Tolstoy thought that the transgression for which Anna was punished was her breaking up a "holy marriage." "Cause" in legal-moral terminology is that which, if demonstrated, leads to certain consequences and punishment. If Tolstoy is right, if Anna's "breaking up a marriage" was a transgression, then in its absence there would have been no punishment: no suffering or death. Let's imagine for a moment that Anna had managed to both continue loving Vronsky and live with her "legitimate" husband, Karenin. We can surmise the effect of this from Tolstoy's description of Anna's relationship with her husband. Right after Anna admits to her husband that she loves Vronsky and Karenin says he would "forget everything if nothing of the kind happened again," she meditates with disgust about her marriage:

"He's in the right!" she muttered. "Of course, he's always in the right; he's a Christian, he's magnanimous! Yes, the mean, odious creature! And no one understands it except me, and no one ever will; and I can't explain it. People say he's so religious, so high-principled, so upright, so clever; but they don't see what I've seen. They don't know how for eight years he has crushed my life, crushed everything that was living in me—he has never once thought that I'm a live woman in need of love. They don't know how at every step he's humiliated me and remained self-satisfied. Haven't I striven, striven with all my might, to find something to give meaning to my life? Haven't I struggled to love him, to love my son when I could no longer love my husband? But the time came when I realized I couldn't deceive myself any longer, that I was alive, that I was not to blame, that God had made me so that I need to love and live. And now what? If he'd killed me, if he'd killed him, I could have borne anything, I could have forgiven anything. But no! He . . ."

But life must go on. Recalling another portion of his letter: "Our life must continue as before . . . ," she thinks how miserable life for her was in the past, and how awful it has been of late and wonders what it can possibly become in the future. A few hours before her death she has a vision:

Thinking of Karenin she immediately saw him before her with extraordinary vividness—the mild, lifeless, faded eyes, the blue veins in his white hands—heard his intonations and the cracking of his finger joints, and remembering the feeling that had once existed between them, and which had also been called love, she shuddered with revulsion. (p. 797)

Marriage with Karenin is torture for Anna. After she meets Vronsky it becomes insurmountable suffering. If, somehow, it had been impossible for Anna to break "the holy marriage," if she had been compelled to stay with her legitimate husband, Karenin, it is obvious that she would have thrown herself under a train a few years sooner than she did. Thus, the reason Tolstoy gives for the transgression and the punishment is not valid, for we do not get rid of final punishment, suffering, and death simply by not acting.

On the other hand, all sociological explanations come down to one fact: society is guilty for Anna's tragedy. Had a more humane social climate surrounded her, i.e., had Anna been able to obtain a legal divorce, there would have been neither the "crucifixion on the cross of maternity and passion" nor the social ostracism that caused her so much suffering. Thus, Anna was punished by a conservative society because she transgressed inhuman and unnatural boundaries.

Several facts in the novel contradict this kind of reasoning.

During the first years of her life with Vronsky, spent mostly abroad, Anna is extremely happy, though her son, Seriozha, is not with her and she feels socially ill-at-ease. When she is about to leave with Vronsky after giving birth to his child, a little girl, in Karenin's home, she refuses to accept a divorce which Karenin offers her because she considers this an unnecessary and superfluous formality. Her happiness is not tainted by thoughts of either her son or her husband's misfortune:

The thought of her husband's misery did not poison her own happiness. On the one hand, that memory was too terrible to dwell on. On the other, what had made her husband unhappy had brought her too much happiness to be the subject of regret. (p. 489)

Anna's suffering begins when her relationship with Vronsky deteriorates. However, she understands that a divorce and custody of her son, which she now unsuccessfully tries to obtain, would not solve anything, i.e., sociological theories would not remove her pain.

> "Suppose I think to myself what it is I want to make me happy. Well? I get a divorce, and Alexei Alexandrovich lets me have Seriozha, and I marry Vronsky. . . . Well, I get divorced, and become Vronsky's wife. What then? Will Kitty cease looking at me as she looked at me today? No. And will Seriozha leave off asking and wondering about my two husbands? And is there any new feeling I can imagine between Vronsky and me? Could there be if not happiness, just absence of torment? No, and no again," she answered herself now without the smallest hesitation. "Impossible! Life is sundering us, and I am the cause of his unhappiness and he of mine, and there's no altering him or me." (p. 797)

Two questions alone—"Will Seriozha leave off asking and wondering about my two husbands? And is there any new feeling I can imagine between Vronsky and me?"—contradict all sociological explanations of Anna's tragedy. In the most humane and perfect society Seriozha would not stop thinking of his mother's two husbands, and Vronsky's feelings would not deepen because of natural law or a more humane "social conscience."

Thus, Anna's suffering is not a result of her transgressing boundaries or her behaving differently from other women. Her distress might have been even greater had she not acted as she did. The cause of her tragedy is not rooted in social norms alone, for nothing would have been solved simply by removing them. Vronsky's love was growing cold and Anna's fear of a second break widened the gap between them. Fear before any event is always the cause of that event. After frequent quarrels, Anna reflects:

> "My love grows more and more passionate and selfish, while his is dying, and that is why we are drifting apart," she went on musing. "And there's no help for it. He is all in all to me, and I demand that he should give himself more and more entirely up to me. And he wants to get farther and farther away from me. Up to the time of our union we were irresistibly drawn apart. And nothing can be done to alter it. He says I am insanely jealous and I have kept on telling myself·that I am insanely jealous; but it is not true. I am not jealous, but unsatisfied. But . . ." Her mouth dropped open and she was so agitated by the sudden thought that came to her that she changed her place in the carriage. "If I could be anything but his mistress, passionately caring for nothing but his caresses—but I can't, and I don't want to be anything else. And my desire arouses his disgust, and that excites resentment in me, and it cannot be otherwise. Don't I know that he wouldn't deceive me, that he has not thought of wanting to marry the Princess Sorokin, that he is not in love with Kitty, that he won't be unfaithful to me? I know all that, but it doesn't make it any the easier for me. If he does not love me, but treats me kindly and gently out of a sense of *duty*, and what I want is not there—that would be a thousand times worse than having him hate me. It would be a hell! And that is just how it is. He has long ceased to love me. And where love ends, hate begins." (p. 796)

Would a divorce, and subsequent marriage to Vronsky have solved anything?

> "If he does not love me, but treats me kindly and gently out of a sense of *duty*, and what I want is not there—that would be a thousand times worse than having him hate me." (p. 796)

Anna tells Vronsky to his face:

"What can I want? All I want is that you should not desert me as you are thinking of doing," she said, understanding all that he had left unsaid. "No, I don't want that . . . that is of secondary importance. I want your love, and it has gone. So it is all over." (p. 777)

"It's love, not the outward form that counts." (p. 780)

N. Gudzy, writing in the *Soviet Encyclopedia* about "the limits of Vronsky's internal image," expresses an already generally accepted opinion that Vronsky, too, is at least partly responsible for the tragedy. Is this really so? Vronsky remains uncompromising to the end, a brave man who sacrifices his career and reputation in society to his love for Anna. He loses just as she does and, after the tragedy, volunteers for the Serbian-Turkish war where he is killed. He cannot be blamed for "limits on an internal image." True, the fact remains that he was growing cool toward Anna, but man is often no master of his feelings. Had he been straightforward Anna might have returned to her "legitimate" husband whom she had tried to love for years. One does not ask a man whether he wishes to love, just as one does not ask whether somebody wishes to be born or not. Let's remember Schopenhauer: "Man can do what he wants or not but he cannot unwish what he really wishes." It is not Anna's fault that she does not love her husband because she loves Vronsky. It is not Vronsky's fault that his love toward Anna cools.

Where, then, is the real root cause of the tragedy? We have shown that neither Leo Tolstoy nor Thomas Mann nor the authors of the encyclopedic essays are right. What could Anna have done to avert tragedy?

Where there is punishment, there is also crime; where there is effect, there is also cause. As Evgeny Minkovsky says: "To explain a phenomenon is to discover its previous existence."

The novel itself provides the answer to the question: What is Anna's sin? Let's carefully read this passage from the novel.

> "I'll begin from the beginning. You married a man twenty years older than yourself. You married him without love, or without knowing what love was. That was a mistake let's admit it."
>
> "A fearful mistake!" said Anna.
>
> "But I repeat—it's an accomplished fact. Then you had, let us say, the misfortune to fall in love with a man not your husband. That was a misfortune, but that, too, is an accomplished fact." (p. 453)

In another place Tolstoy presents the origin of Anna's dilemma:

> During the time when he was the governor, Anna's aunt, a rich provincial lady, introduced the man, not young any more, but a young (new) governor, to her cousin and led him to a situation when he had either to propose to the girl or to leave the town. Alexei Alexandrovich could not make up his mind for a long time. There were as many reasons then, for that step as against it, and there was not a decisive motive, which would make him change his rule: temperance in doubt. But Anna's aunt let him know through some acquaintances that he had already compromised the girl, and that his honor obliged him to propose. So he did and offered his fiancee and wife all the sentiments he was capable to give.

Doesn't the key to the whole tragedy lie in the fact that Anna, like most girls of her class, married without love? Didn't everything follow from this fact? As a normal woman, she had to fall in love at least once in her life. Nobody could guarantee that she would fall in love with her future husband. All tragedy and suffering was only an emotional consequence of Anna's complying with social norms, of her marriage without love.

Had she had a normal marriage with Vronsky, the man she loved, the cooling of his affections would not have caused the tragedy which came to Anna, the tragedy of a mother who never loved the father of her child, the tragedy of a passionate young woman whom fate condemns to be the lover but never the wife of a man whose child she bears. Let's remember:

> "If I could be anything but his mistress, passionately caring for nothing but his caresses—but I can't, and I don't want to be anything else."

Had there been no marriage with Karenin, had she not had a child with a man she never loved, there would have been no tragedy. It's all Anna's fault. Society is guilty insofar as it tolerated marriages without love although, one has to admit, that society never compelled Anna to marry Karenin. She could have resisted and not acted as "all others."

The purpose of this essay is not to show that efforts to create a more humane and progressive society are useless. Rather it is to point out that in "the realm of freedom," the responsibility of the individual (and tragedy, i.e., punishment for transgression) can be incomparably greater because of greater freedom for the personality. Only in this sense can one understand Dostoyevsky's defending "the right to suffer" as a defense of freedom itself. This much is clear: Where there is no freedom of choice, there is no responsibility or punishment. By punishment we naturally do not mean death, but mental suffering, that medieval "last judgment" from which Anna flees to her death. There would have been no such suffering had personal guilt not existed. Many times in history strong and great men have perished and lost their battles within a conservative environment, but their deaths were not the consequence of mental suffering and were not accompanied by it. We have only to think of numberless revolutionaries who, shortly before they died, amazed their contemporaries with their deep faith in the triumph of justice on earth and their spiritual peace. Conformity, betrayal of oneself, is always accompanied by mental anguish and self-destruction. Anna Karenina was no revolutionary. She was punished for her conformity, for her self-betrayal, in marrying Karenin. The rest is only consequence. Nothing later succeeds in restoring her defiant attitude toward society.

Who really punishes Anna? Not society, because years of social ostracism could not spoil her happiness with Vronsky. Not Vronsky, because he cools toward her only when it is clear to him that Anna is not the mother of his child but only his mistress.

We have emphasized that Tolstoy is closer to the truth than those who resort to sociological explanations. If we replace Tolstoy's "holy marriage," a formula based on religion and law, with spontaneous, natural love and passion that man cannot control, just as he cannot control natural forces, then Tolstoy is right. The breakup of "a holy marriage"—not of social norms but of natural love, of the psychophysical links between two people—is the sin for which Anna was punished. Her marriage to Karenin and her bearing his son constitute the transgression of what Tolstoy calls "holy marriage."

But we are still left with the question: Who punishes Anna? To answer it we must appeal to the findings of psychology and medicine. Several years ago doctors in the United States were studying families of psychologically retarded children. They discovered that lack of love between the parents was an essential trait common to these families even though the parents often successfully concealed this fact from the children. The doctors found that mentally healthy, normal children come from "natural marriages," i.e., those based exclusively on spontaneous common feelings and sympathies between parents. That concealing the lack of love between parents does not help (i.e., the psychological development of the child is deeply disturbed whether parents hide the fact or not) shows that psychic bonds between parents—their love—are meaningfully real. (Perhaps in the distant future the psychological energy of love will be measurable with precise devices.) Most interesting, perhaps, is the fact that children from divorced families accepted as their father the man with whom their mother sympathized, whereas they remained quite indifferent to their real father.

What we call moral sin, moral punishment, remorse, etc., is often no more than the psychosomatic reaction of an organism, made up of physical and psychic parts. One way or another conformity is ultimately severely punished. Conformity is basically the submission and the subjection of the natural aspirations of an individual, psychological "I" to outside forces, usually to transient and obsolete social norms. Every "I" really contains in itself a multifaceted psychic or physical "We" of the future which over time is no less real than the transient "We" of the present which is but a cross-section of life. The society of today is only a slice through humanity, organically, not mechanistically, speaking: man is never just a social being but an individual as well if we mean, by individual, the future. The sacrifice of the individual (the future) to society (the present) is what we call conformity.

Anna, then, was punished by her individual subconsciousness. Dostoyevsky would say that Anna punished herself, i.e., that she was punished by an eternity of "I's" which she carried in herself. The exact terms are not essential. There is no essential difference between the confession in church and psychoanalytic therapy. Social forms, norms, and laws are only a reflection of real connections among men; the evil begins when these reflections are taken as the only reality. Socially legitimate marriage is but a confirmation of a psychological connection between two people. This confirmation without the connection produces a lie of conformity and violence for which both the person that commits the violence and the one that suffers it are responsible.

Thus, Anna's psychological afflictions are completely justified and natural, as natural as physical pain caused by a hot iron.

In the publication *Russian Archives* for the year 1868 an article by Leo Tolstoy was printed under the title "A Few Words about the Book *War and Peace*." There the great writer, though he does not give his obviously naive explanations for historical events in this novel, does answer his critics (Turgenev among others) who complained that he did not sufficiently voice "the spirit of the times":

> To that criticism I answer as follows: I am quite aware of those burning questions which they cannot find in my novel: the horrors of serfdom, the immurement of women in the foundations of walls, the whipping of grown-up sons, Saltichikha,* etc.; these "trends of the times," which live in our imagination I do not regard as accurate and I did not want to express them. Studying letters, diaries, and legends I have found no more horrors of that madness than I find nowadays or in any other epoch. During those times men were loving and envying, searching for truth and mercy; they were filled with passions; intellectual and moral life was as complicated, or even more refined, than it is in today's high society. If an opinion was formed in our set of notions about the spirit of self-will and oppression of those times, this is because in the legends, notes, stories, and novels only the most extreme cases of tyranny and self-will reached us.

In essence, Tolstoy here opposes sociological vulgarization according to which every historical period must conform to its

---

Saltichikha—a historical character, the lady of a manor, who acquired a bad reputation because of her sadistic tortures of her serfs.

socioeconomic characteristics in order to create a so-called contemporary spirit. Are the Middle Ages really only a period of darkness? The Renaissance, a period of "awakening"? The capitalistic epoch, a time of merciless exploitation? The time is ripe for introducing integrals and differentials into the rough algebra of sociology. Pascal was quite serious when he wrote in his *Pensees:* "If Cleopatra's nose were longer or shorter by a millimeter, world history would have traveled a different course." Naturally, this is only a slightly exaggerated example upholding an opinion that historical movements often depend on minimal factors. Not by chance did Pascal become one of the inventors of differential calculus.

We have tried to show in this short essay how wrong rough sociological generalizations can be. We chose Anna Karenina because, at first glance, her fate seems to illustrate sociological theories.

Together with the humanization of social relationships and the liberation of man, the individual's responsibility increases, which means that conformity will result in harsher chastisement and no idealized Communist society can give man happiness without extorting a price.

Only there, in "our homeland" as Ernest Bloch would say, would Anna Karenina be fully responsible for her sin; only there would Anna's crime and punishment be properly understood and freed of the burden of sociological theory.

Yugoslavia, 1963

NOTES

1. Thomas Mann, *Essays on Three Decades* (New York: Alfred A. Knopf, 1948), p. 184.
2. A. V. Lunacharsky, *About Russian Literature* (Belgrade: 1959).

Mystical Experiences of the Labor Camps

> *An individual need not defend God,*
> *for God defends the individual, or,*
> *in other words, it is not necessary*
> *to defend God but to seek Him.* [1]

Lev Shestov

> *As he loved cursing, so let it come*
> *unto him: as he delighted not in*
> *blessing, so let it be far from him.*

Psalms 109:17

In recent years, numerous books written by people who have passed through Soviet camps and prisons have appeared. All aspects of prison existence are thoroughly described in these books. Several eyewitness accounts attract special attention, because they show not only the physical side of prison life but also the most profound emotional and spiritual experiences and transformations undergone by those who have passed through the terrifying world of Soviet prisons and camps.

In these descriptions of emotional and spiritual experiences, much appears paradoxical from the customary contemporary viewpoint. However, since people whose world views and perceptions are completely *different* have nonetheless indisputably attested to the *identical* processes that transpire in the depths of the human soul and, at the same time, have affirmed and described the *dependence* of human fate on these deeply internal processes, it is therefore possible to try to systematize and understand their paradoxical evidence.

This article was translated by Alexey A. Kiselev

The authors often adhere to philosophical and religious views directly opposed to the experience they describe; and if it is difficult for those who have undergone total deprivation of freedom to come to appropriate conclusions, then for people who have never had such experiences these conclusions, as well as the facts described in their books, will obviously seem incomprehensible.

One must emphasize from the outset that the phenomena to be analyzed are revolutionary, not only in relation to the psychology and psychoanalysis of the twentieth century, but also to Marxism in contemporary Western sociology. More importantly, though, they explode the very foundations on which modern science and philosophy are built. It should be repeated that in discussing empirical phenomena recorded by people who have nothing in common, the duplication of experience and evidence is so much more weighty and valuable.

In view of this, it appears that the books of the following authors are the most interesting ones: Solzhenitsyn's first and second volume of *The Gulag Archipelago*[2]; Shifrin's *In the Fourth Dimension*[3]; Panin's *Notes of Sologdin*[4]; and *Voice from the Crowd*, by Synavsky-Tertz.[5] Grossman's *Forever Flowing*[6] is also interesting inasmuch as it contains perhaps one of the first attempts to comprehend the terrible experience of loss of freedom. This author, however, did not personally experience the world he describes. Therefore we will not refer to his work as a first-hand account.

Many other well-known books about the Soviet prison world are irrelevant to the problem at hand, for in these works—as in many analogous accounts about German concentration camps—most of the attention is devoted to a description of the material world of imprisonment. These include a spectrum of works from Ivan Solonevich's "Russia in a Concentration Camp" and Margolin's "In the Land of Zek" to Eugenia Ginzburg's *Journey into the Whirlwind*, the accounts of Soviet authors which are published in the Soviet Union—as, for example, those of General Gorbatov, numerous accounts of Western authors (such as Weisberg-Tsibulskii, Margareta Bubber-Naimann, etc.), Varga's "Life under Prison Guard," the book by Marchenko, and even earlier works of Solzhenitsyn.

FUNDAMENTAL PARADOXES

In the previously mentioned books of Solzhenitsyn, Panin, Shifrin, and Tertz, several continually repeated paradoxical statements immediately impress the thoughtful reader. All these authors agree that arrest, prison, and camp—simply to say, the loss of freedom—have formed the most profound and significant experience in their lives. The paradox is complicated by the fact that, although they underwent the most extreme spiritual and physical suffering during their imprisonment, they also experienced a fulfilling happiness, undreamed of by people outside the prison walls.

None of these authors had ever before experienced such powerful feelings of love, hate, or despair, such days and nights filled with the most profound questions concerning human life, nor felt so close to the essence of cosmic life. Thus their descriptions of imprisonment are descriptions of an intense, concentrated life . . . a life, which despite all torment, was oddly precious. Suicide, in general, was rare.[7] Least suitable for these documents by former prisoners is the name given by Dostoyevsky during his time to *Notes from the House of the Dead*. Or, more precisely, under conditions of incredibly severe stress from the external, physical environment—*which is the loss of freedom* and which is very rarely found in normal life—a fundamental division of people into the living and the dead occurs. The latter are those who are spiritually dead while physically living, and only in relation to them may the term "House of the Dead" be applied. In the words of Shifrin, "In these conditions there was no middle ground. A person either broke or grew stronger.[8]

Also striking is the paradoxical assertion and the empirical evidence that the body—the physical being—saved that individual who redeemed his soul . . . who, in the name of an internal imperative, was prepared to sacrifice his body and physical life.

We usually think just the reverse, that is, that a person in difficult circumstances is faced with a choice between salvation either of the body or of the soul. But those having gone through the most adverse circumstances, which threatened both soul and body, unanimously affirm that those who have sacrificed their soul to save their body have lost both; while for those who were prepared to sacrifice their body to save their soul, some kind of strange and mysterious law, eluding understanding, preserved both.

Thus, regardless of how powerful might be those forces which set as their goal the destruction of both the spirit and the body of a human being, *life experience* has revealed to us that deep in the human soul is an unfamiliar force which is stronger than all the external forces of enslavement and death. This force is stronger, not in a symbolic sense, but in an actual, empirical sense. People who have witnessed this phenomenon arrive at a conviction about the power of psychic energy contained in the soul of each human being. These witnesses describe this phenomenon as a fact—proven hundreds of times—which repeats itself during the terrible circumstances of imprisonment. They manifest the inseparability of the spiritual from the physical world, and indicate that a person's thoughts and aspirations are not less, but on the contrary, much more active in the external, physical world than his hands.

At the same time, these witnesses insist on the fact that nothing in their lives occurred by mere fortuity. On the contrary, they insist that everything occurred by means of some unknown fate, which pulled and drove them along a definite road—against their own plans and attempts to change their own destiny. Here we find what appears to be a contradiction: on the one hand, we find some unknown forces within man which by some mysterious means are at times extraordinary in their action in the physical world. On the other hand, a certain fatalism and determinism exists, which man is incapable of changing.

However, this contradiction is only apparent. If a person follows the deeply rooted voice of his soul—which is not subject to any rational control, acting contrary to all exterior circumstances, contrary to his desires and plans, contrary to the threat of physical destruction, contrary to arguments and decisions of his intellect and the views of public opinion—then new courses open up in the life of such a person, by inertia, which lead to the preservation of all that had been sacrificed during the process of following this mystical compass. Even more, the most cherished spiritual aspirations are realized.

If, however, a person, through his actions in the external world, in defiance to the deeply rooted voice of his soul (which we shall call the instinct of freedom), attempts to realize his desires and plans, to preserve his life and avoid destruction— fate enters into play precisely at that time, the fate which will lead sooner or later to the destruction of that for which the person rejected the voice of his soul to achieve.

And man is free with respect to whether or not to follow this mysterious, yet extremely real, calling of his internal voice. More precisely, it should be said that a person *becomes free* after having experienced the suffering and mastering the terrible lessons of captivity.

Therefore, there is no contradiction. Both fate, which cannot be changed, and unlimited freedom, which goes so far as to determine the physical conditions under which a person lives, exist simultaneously in the world. Thus, it depends on man himself whether or not he will live in the bond of fate or in freedom, which is independent of the physical laws of the world.

Certainly, if everything is as stated and the accounts about which we are speaking bear witness to it, then its far-reaching conclusions undermine the ground on which all the foundations of science rest, not only with regard to man and the human soul, but with regard to all reality, both visible and invisible. If two worlds exist simultaneously, unblendable but also inseparable, i.e., the world of absolute fate and the world of freedom, and if people live in one or the other of these two worlds depending on their following or repudiation of that completely solitary and individualized, as well as mysterious, internal voice (which at times is not too audible)—then all science becomes superficial. This internal voice is not subject to any intellectual criteria or scientific study, since the point of departure of science is the premise of the existence of only one world, ruled over specifically by the cognition of laws independent of man. To those people who have gone through the focused life, the experience of the life of captivity attests to quite the opposite. Even the recognition of these mysterious, unknown laws that have saved those who have followed the command of that internal voice in contradiction to the visible and self-evident horrors they experienced—and notwithstanding the knowledge of those laws contemporary science is studying—has shown that it offered them no power. And indeed no power is needed, for it is not power that saves one, but freedom. And this freedom gives *not knowledge, but faith*, without which it is impossible to follow what is not substantiated by anything "objective"—i.e., one's inner voice. Or to state it more precisely: the following of this internal voice *is faith*.

Here, in this concentrated life, an "experiment of the doctrine, amidst those terrible conditions" is being conducted, as Panin writes.[9] "Here, one thinks much more intensely than in the world of scholarship," Synavsky-Tertz states,[10] and as a result of his personal existential experience he arrives at a categorical assertion that "science separates itself from the truth."[11] For this reason, the prisoners read hand-copied passages from the Bible and the New Testament with intensity. Through personal experience, they rediscover the fundamental treatises of the Eastern teachings of Yoga, which have been forgotten by people of modern times. They approach the elementary truths of theosophy. They try with all their might to comprehend their own experience, which is not subject to any doubts and which renders obsolete a whole range of teachings, ideologies, doctrines, and science of our times.

And here is perhaps the most paradoxical and optimistic conviction of those people, who have themselves experienced the full force of evil on their own backs. This conviction is that the force of goodness is unconquerable, as Panin writes,[12] that the world more resembles a white tablecloth with a few specks of black evil, and not the reverse, as Shifrin assures us,[13] that the executioner executes himself, while the one who is to be destroyed remains alive, to use the words of Grossman,[14] that "life is much more significant than we think," as Tertz insists.[15]

IT IS NOT A POLITICAL MATTER

From everything that has been mentioned so far, it is seen

that the struggle taking place between man and the forces of evil and death (about which the books to which we have made references speak with such spiritual clearsightedness) is, least of all, a strictly political struggle. On the surface, it indeed appears that the discussion here centers on political collisions, that we speak about the rule of a one-party dictatorship, about the tyranny and uncontrolled practices of political police, about the lack of legal rights and freedom of speech. However, this is only the perceived side and social projection of a different struggle. This harsh and severe struggle is taking place in the depths of innumerable human souls placed in a situation in which it is impossible to avoid participating. It is impossible to avoid making this fatal choice: to submit to the powerful—and to this day, victorious—rule, force, and coercion, or else to stand up against it, i.e., to put one's faith, with no guarantees, in the existing internal voice.

Consequently, the struggle which is occurring today in totalitarian countries is not, in essence, a political struggle, but rather a religious struggle. This, certainly, is not always realized even by the participants themselves in this great battle. Solzhenitsyn writes with complete justification that it is specifically the Christians in the USSR who are truly political,[16] in the sense that it is they who undermine the very essence of totalitarian rule, i.e., the belief in the unlimited power of external circumstances, which supposedly direct man's inner world (i.e., his soul).

If the external world is invincible, then human slavery cannot be eliminated by any political reforms. If, however, the opposite is true, if *the physical world is subject to the spiritual forces of the human soul,* then man's fate depends entirely on himself. From this, we may conclude that there are none who suffer who are innocent and that all ordeals and torments are deserved and rightful. In this case, the road opens up for a free life, in which the human political system appears only as a consequence of the spiritual liberation of one's soul.

For the majority of people, the question of whether or not man is dependent on the external world or, conversely, the physical world is dependent on man is, generally speaking, a strictly theoretical question. However, the people whose works we are analyzing were placed in a situation where they, together with millions of others, had to resolve this question, since it was of great importance to their own human existence and hence had a *particularly practical meaning* to them. To answer this question meant to live or to die—not in a figurative sense, but in a literal sense. Following the mysterious callings of his internal voice—redeeming his soul—man arrived at an empirical cognition that as long as the soul is not forfeited, the fundamental part is not lost—and this is the basis on which the belief in the immortality of the human soul rests. To follow the calling of one's internal voice means to qualify all of one's deeds of time in relation to eternity.

However, this trial is of extraordinary importance not only for the people who were placed in a situation of maximum nonfreedom, but for all people who lived in the past or who are living on the face of the earth today. It is very important to understand that sooner or later *every human being* will find himself in a prison, in a detention camp, or under the unlimited, arbitrary rule of the mighty physical forces of this world. Then it is impossible to avoid the choice between submission before death—total destruction not only physically but also spiritually; or, in contradiction to everything "real," objective, and sensible, to follow, in a daring way, the calling of the spiritual voice. Sickness, different catastrophes, various misfortunes, death—all of these are the very same as arrest, inquisition, prison, detention camp. *And it is not given to anyone to avoid them.*

Although people who have not gone through the experience

of incarceration assume that there is a significant difference between the existence inside the prison or outside the prison walls, those who did go through the experience of incarceration have begun to understand that the difference is only superficial and temporary. For in one unexpected moment for every human being the world of freedom appears as in the cell of a prisoner condemned to death. "Our whole world is a prison cell of those condemned to death"[17] is how Solzhenitsyn describes it, and he goes on to say that "the cell is crammed, but is not free will even more crammed?"[18] Panin substantiates that "the whole world is only a point of departure,"[19] while Tertz likens death to an exiting into freedom."[20]

THE FIRST AND MOST IMPORTANT

What happens within a person at that moment when, suddenly torn out of an ordinary life, he is thrust under the jurisdiction of merciless and powerful forces which appear to have only one wish—his destruction? Is any kind of defense or resistance possible? Everything a person had lived by, everything he possessed, i.e., free will, people who were close to him, work which he enjoyed, private property, his physical being, his life—none of these is he able to defend, and all is in the hands of the forces of evil. And if a person attempts to resist in the sphere of that by which, until this time, he had lived and possessed, he is doomed to defeat from the very outset. The person *himself* is in no way capable of defending anything that the powerful external forces, in whose grip he is now placed, wish to take away.

Thus finding himself on the edge of an abyss, a person, before complete destruction, begins to understand that nevertheless something exists which is not within the realm of

Underground Notes

the external, invincible forces. And even though all the rest can no longer be saved, resistance, fight, and victory are possible in one way: in the preservation of the soul—or to put it another way, which is, however, *exactly the same thing*—in safeguarding one's spiritual freedom and in resistance to evil and force. However, in order for this fight to be successful or even possible, one must renounce, beforehand, everything that the physical forces can take away.

"Only do not value life,"[21] writes Solzhenitsyn, adding: don't have anything, renounce even your own body.[22] Renounce everything, for even people who are close to you are your enemies.[23] And Panin underscores this by attesting that in order to fight, it is essential to renounce even those who are close to you[24]—to renounce everything under the sun except the soul. And only through this complete renunciation does a person become free—only then, when he no longer has anything to lose.[25]

And at that instant when this occurs, and the person becomes totally free, then in the experience of people who underwent this concentrated form of life, i.e., the maximum of nonfreedom, the most mysterious aspect of their trial occurs: some kind of all-powerful force appears in the depths of their soul. This force not only gives the mutilated body an incredible ability for resistance, but by some kind of utterly mystical means—which our present-day consciousness is unable to fully explain—begins to influence the external world . . . let us repeat again: to influence and determine events which to our present-day consciousness appear to be independent of man, yet are nevertheless a saving force for him.

Because of this, Panin kept repeating, "redeem your soul, and you will save your body."[26] Only the spirit saves, the spirit supports the body, as Solzhenitsyn states many times.[27] They both describe what they experienced personally or else witnessed with their own eyes: the incredible tenacity of a body possessed by strong internal spiritual intensity. And the same holds true in the reverse—they have witnessed on numerous occasions how the loss of spirituality led directly to physical death.

RELATION TO THE SPIRITUAL FORCE

There is an enormous force hidden inside us, exclaims Panin, and he goes on to say that the whole universal system of condensation and discharge is tied, by some mysterious threads, with the depths of our spirit.[28] Solzhenitsyn states that each one of us is the center of the universe.[29] And it is not through some abstract means that they have come to this conclusion, but on numerous occasions they experienced the action of this unknown force on their own backs. Solzhenitsyn attests to a mysterious inner warmth which appeared as though from another world and saved a man in an icebox isolator.[30] Panin tells of an incomprehensible and unknown force which brought him back to life after forty days' oblivion, and he goes on narrating about a prisoner who rolled daily in the snow, stark naked, during bitter, freezing weather—without any harm to his health. Those witness accounts attest to many incomprehensible and striking events which they have either gone through themselves or borne witness to.

When the individual threw everything physical aside and decided to follow the internal voice—which in itself is *faith* —he suddenly saw and felt in himself, quite empirically with joy, horror, and trepidation, this mysterious but at the same time real and powerful force which acted both in his body and in the external world. And simultaneously with this came the realization that he is not the owner of this force, i.e., that it is not his prerogative to direct it according to his own judgment, but on the contrary, that everything in life—and life itself—

is completely dependent upon this spiritual and mysterious force (*mistikos*—which is, mystic) and, in the *language of religion*, it is called God.

This lived-through experiencing of an all-powerful unknown force led the prisoners toward their attempts to comprehend and perceive both this mysterious force itself as well as man's relationship to it . . . not to study this problem in an abstract way, or in a theoretical way, or in an experimental way in an attempt to reach a "scientific" goal—none of these. They had only a single goal: to be saved from the terrible but unavoidable threat of death. Both prayers and meditation, as well as the technique of Yoga, and even simple exorcism, were tested and subject to verification. Not only the Old and New Testaments—found written down on small scraps of paper, recorded by memory—but also everything bound with the ancient teaching of Yoga, with parapsychology, with theosophy, appeared as the most essential and necessary *practical* means for the protection of both the soul and the body. Under such circumstances, the action of the spirit triggered a direct effect, seen by people with their own eyes, on the physical world.

Panin, who also writes about Raja-yoga,[31] attests to the true power of prayer.[32] Shifrin writes about Hatha-yoga,[33] about the "secret doctrine" of Blavatsky,[34] about camp samizdat on the subject of parapsychology,[35] and so on. Once again, truths long forgotten over many centuries of history became self-evident: that the air is simultaneously the spirit which is nourished with energies unknown to us, using the words of Tertz[36]; that the food consumed by man contains a mysterious and life-giving energy, which the ancient Indians called prana[37]; that man is being protected, in a quite positive way, from outside evil as well as from physical pain, by means of celestial armor, as related by Panin, who had experienced such a defense himself.[38] And Solzhenitsyn says that under pressure of both physical and spiritual suffering, a person loses the "coat of mail of evil energy."[39]

It is quite understandable that people who experienced mysterious and terrifying phenomena also experienced, not by their own choosing, confusion about numerous religious, mystical, magical, esoteric theories and doctrines. Moreover, the minds of those people have been cultivated in an entirely materialistic environment and even in a technical education. Because of this, we should not be surprised by such an expression, for example, as that of Panin, that spiritual energy, in a manner analagous to electricity, is used up either in the work of the intellect or else during manual physical labor.[40] Similarly, the theory of the sun's activity as a source of influence on the management of revolutions on this earth is *accepted quite naturally.* [41] And even the magical influence of the mere mention of the name of Jesus Christ on the instruments of force, as Solzhenitsyn writes,[42] is also *accepted quite naturally.*

Nevertheless, in spite of all attempts toward a theoretical understanding, it became apparent that no spiritual technique could be developed to control this mysterious force. It was guiding and showing the way to people by unknown and spiritual signs which not everyone was able to recognize. And one could either commit oneself to this force or refuse to. But it was impossible to direct this mystical force by one's own desire or wish, and all one could do was take directions from it.

THE SPIRITUAL EYE
(Oculus Spiritualis)

Solzhenitsyn admirably describes an internal "relay," which flawlessly foretold him about man—with whom he had to deal in the course of his life.[43] Others also attest to the flawlessness of that which we have become accustomed to calling intuition. The singular physical manifestation of the spiritual world of man was his eyes. On numerous occasions, Shifrin,[44] Panin,[45] and Solzhenitsyn[46] attested to the fact that eyes speak "better than the passport." What then is the only relayable criterion of truth which cannot be rationally taught nor which man is able to express in words? And here we see that experience has shown that specifically the spiritual eye is the one and only true criterion in this world.

But it was not only when in direct contact with people that the spiritual "relay" faultlessly told man about the deep-rooted existence of different phenomena. There was also that which we call presentiment which, acting from a distance, gave a completely accurate announcement to man about danger, success, and about all events which touched his life. Panin tells of the deadly melancholy that he experienced at that moment when the decision was made to arrest him, as he found out later.[47] An intuitive feeling clearly told Panin that on that day his food ration, which he left in the barrack, would be stolen (which under those conditions was a threat on one's life).[48] Solzhenitsyn tells of the premonition of trouble by a runaway prisoner, who was traveling to get his wife and was saved only because he entrusted himself entirely to that inner feeling and changed his plans.[49] We find many similar empirical eyewitness accounts in the books we are analyzing.

Therefore, there is some kind of cosmic, absolute communion of human souls—however, not only cosmic but also a communion outside the time scope—about which people who themselves have experienced such an occurrence bear witness. Solzhenitsyn describes a foreseer, who was in the same cell with him and who unmistakably saw in his dreams all the most important events which were to take place in the cell the next day.[50] After his release, Shifrin even set out on a long journey to a foreseer,[51] because after the experience he had survived the possibility of vision outside time and space had become so clear to him.

Synavsky-Tertz, who went through comparatively mild trials during the post-Stalin period, was better prepared spiritually than others, prior to prison, for the discernment of mystical phenomena. He writes about how questions to which one is constantly seeking an answer are suddenly solved,[52] and he tells how books for which he had a need were passed to him, as if by an invisible hand, at the most needful moment. One's thought is no less potent than physical action, as Shifrin states,[53] and he tells of incidents when something would invariably lead him, when he was tormented with insoluble questions, into a face-to-face meeting with a strange theosophist prisoner who suddenly approached him during one of the deportation trips and familiarized him with esoteric philosophies,[54] or about his sudden receipt of occult books while in the hospital.

Out of the realization that thought by itself is effectual, it becomes explicable why, in totalitarian systems, the most terrible crime is "different thinkingness," to use Shifrin's words.[55] Or, as Solzhenitsyn writes, "it was only thought that was punished."[56]

Nevertheless, precisely the incidents our authors use to illustrate the efficacy of thought indicate that it was not thought, but something else, that was extremely active. Thought by itself in the internal world—like the books and necessary meetings in the external world—were only pushed toward the person by someone at the needful moment. The best example of this, which fully illustrates the most important, fundamental mystical law, is given in a story told by Solzhenitsyn about an incident concerning an imprisoned astrophysicist, presented in the first book of *Gulag*.[57] The astrophysicist, being held in solitary confinement, was protecting himself from insanity by intensively solving some profound astrophysical problems. However, after a certain time lapse he encountered an obstacle he couldn't overcome: he could not recall certain data and numbers needed for his work. This intense work of his mind, through which the astrophysicist was protecting himself, came to an end. In desperation he began to cry out in anguish, not knowing to whom to appeal for rescue—either to God or to some unknown force. And it was here that a true miracle occurred: in error, entirely by coincidence, an astrophysics manual was delivered to his cell from the prison library. He could not have imagined the existence of such a manual on these premises. Even though in the span of two days the error had been discovered and the manual taken away, the astrophysicist was nevertheless able to search out and remember all the data necessary to continue his mental work and to create a new and original theory.

Shifrin, also, describes incidents of mysterious interferences in the flow of events that were threatening the most important thing in his life, to which all his spiritual strivings were directed. Due to a few extraordinary strokes of luck, a single copy of the Bible and a handwritten text of "Exodus" had been saved during detention camp searches. Shifrin had dedicated much of his energy to the translation and circulation of "Exodus."[58]

It was not thought which was operative, but the complete spiritual, internal striving toward a specific goal. It, in turn, provoked a response of the mystical force in the external world—which is supposedly a world independent of man. It is not thought which is operative, nor the magic power of thought over the environment, but rather that the "heavens were listening to the prayers and were interfering,"[59] as Solzhenitsyn conjectures in his second book of *Gulag*.

Therefore, one may say that the punishment of any kind of dissent under a totalitarian regime is not the reason for the dissent, but rather its result, because it is a physical sign of one's inner striving toward some kind of goal. This striving is threatening to authority by the mere fact that it is spiritual, which means that it is free of the jurisdiction of the ruler of the physical world. It is not thought that is being punished, but the spiritual striving.

The strong spiritual striving elicits events in the physical world which open up the opportunity for fulfillment of this inner striving. Or, more precisely, the strong spiritual striving elicits the response of the mystical force which is located both in the depths of the human soul and in the external world. Thus it appears to man that at the needful moment someone interferes in the flow of life and helps to reach the goal, to achieve that to which the inner striving is directed. This, therefore, is the basic mystical law which changes the entire construction of human thinking, and explodes the foundations on which the principles of science rest.

However, it should be said right from the outset that this spiritual striving we are speaking about is not a striving directed by one's will, and it is not subordinate to man's desires or preferences. The only thing that man can direct is a decision of whether or not to follow those spiritual inclinations. However, in regard to the physical world, the act of following the inner voice wherever it may call one to go is an act of the greatest freedom. One recalls the words of Berdyaev, who said that it is not man who wishes freedom, but rather God who demands that man be free.

In modern Western literature there is a work which very well illustrates this mystical law concerning the interrelation of the physical and spiritual worlds. This is a story by the known French writer, Verkor, which describes a young Rumanian who was in love with the French culture, the French language, and with France itself. He, obeying an inner striving, contrary to any rational decision, left his friends and relatives, his job and his country, and went to Paris, where he didn't know a single person except for some distant relative whose address this young man didn't know. However, in this huge, unfamiliar city, an inner calling led him to one of the Seine River bridges about which he had read while still in Rumania. And quite "accidentally," on that very day and at that very hour, something led his relative to the very same bridge. This opened up the opportunity for this young man to live in France, as well as to fulfill all his sacred dreams.

The actualization of the true connection of man's physical world with that of the spiritual world is religion (*religio* means bond, connection). Faith is that following of the inner voice without the sanction of the intellect, regardless of wherever it might summon one.

I have already written about this basic law of the dependence of the external world on the internal world, of the physical world on the spiritual, while hints concerning this can be found in the Russian samizdat literature of recent times.[60] The comments and reviews concerning this work of mine indicate the nonunderstanding of the essence of the subject which I discussed.[61] An opinion was expressed that the fundamental mystical law about which I was writing is identical to the ideas expressed by Romano Guardini in his outstanding book about Dostoyevsky. This is incorrect. It is specifically Guardini who is far from understanding the law about which I have written in the past with regard to samizdat, and with regard to empirical testimony presented in the books of Solzhenitsyn, Panin, Shifrin, and Tertz.

Guardini's discussion centers on the idea that people live in different worlds, depending on the spiritual world of the individual. However, this is, for example, only in the sense that entirely different wide roads and opportunities materialize for a good person, a happy person, a person whose heart is open in love for all living beings than for a person who is angry and hates both himself and the whole world. Before the former, all humanity and animals and even plants open up to him and even reach out to him, while for the latter, they flee from him. This means that people live in one world or another depending on their hearts. For the former, the world in which he lives will be free, open, while for the latter, it will in many instances be unfree and closed up.

There is nothing mystical in Guardini's conclusions, and even modern psychology can easily substantiate the occurrences which he describes. I, on the other hand, am speaking all the while about something else . . . about the real influence of man's spiritual world upon events which are completely independent of one another, in the physical sense and in the sense of space, such as those described by Solzhenitsyn, Tertz, Shifrin, and Verkor. The astrophysics manual which "accidentally" appeared in the prisoner's cell was the result of his inner striving, not of personal fascination or contacts. The Parisian relative of the young Rumanian was "accidentally" crossing the bridge on that day and at that hour when the Rumanian went there. He went there because he was led by a mystical force, which was spurred into action through the process of following the inner calling on the part of his young relative. This has nothing in common with that about which Guardini speaks in his book on Dostoyevsky.

At the same time it must be emphasized that it was not I who first spoke about this fundamental mystical law. To the best of my knowledge, the first one ever to write specifically about this phenomenon, even though not using the term "law," was Georgii Meyer, in his superb book, *Light in the Night*, which was an analysis of Dostoyevsky's *Crime and Punishment*. [62] In general, it is interesting to note how little known this profound book is in comparison to the popular books about Dostoyevsky by historians and literary theoreticians as, for example, the book by Bakhtin[63]—which appears simply as spiritual rubbish.

The fundamental mystical law indicates that an unknown common basis for both the physical and the spiritual world exists, and that occurrences in the physical world depend on occurrences in the spiritual world—not the other way around. And once again, the words from the Ancient Book become clear that the physical world rests on ten righteous people—not in a figurative sense, but quite literally. And from this, it follows that perhaps the stories from this Ancient Book which describe incidents when the laws of nature and of the physical world yielded to man, and not he to them, are not an empty fantasy.

EVERYTHING IS CORRECT

However, if everything that happens to a person during his lifetime is simply the result of his relationship to the spiritual world, then does it follow that prisons, detention camps, and all suffering are deserved and quite in conformity with the established law? Yes, that this is precisely so is stipulated through their experience by those who underwent the maximum of nonfreedom. At the same time, are there those who were punished without being guilty, who followed the inner voice precisely and were brought to the gates of death because of their resistance to violence? This is also true, our authors affirm. Here again we see a clear contradiction, which we witness through our own experience in life. What can be done?

Consequently, Solzhenitsyn makes a reservation in his second book of *Gulag* that with regard to himself he totally accepts the fact that everything which happened to him was entirely deserved (not only prison and the concentration camp, but also his grave illness). However, he does not choose to extend this principle to those who have not resigned themselves to the powers of force, nor sold out their soul, but who nevertheless perished in the "Archipelago."

One recalls "The Death of Ivan Ilych," in which Tolstoy, describing the unbearable spiritual suffering of the dying man, says that at a specific moment Ivan Ilych understood that, in itself, death is not frightening. The main and fundamental basis of his suffering is buried in the type of life he led. He lived in sin—obviously not with regard to the commonly accepted moral and ethical norms, but in relationship to the inner voice, that voice about which we are speaking. And Ivan Ilych felt during his hour of death that the only real relief came to him in rare moments of his life when he was following the inner voice, and not the popularly accepted opinions and customs, for example, some kind of youthful love, friendship. . . .

This very same thing is substantiated in the experiences of those who survived the maximum loss of freedom. It was not the imprisonment that was frightening, but the life led prior to the arrest! On numerous occasions they all, especially Solzhenitsyn in *Gulag*, describe that spiritual suffering which was brought out through the recollection of preprison life, about sinning with respect to one's own soul—which meant sinning with respect to other people as well.

However, certainly none of us is to avoid death, for it awaits also those who have survived inquisition, prison, and concentration camp through the miracle of the mystical law. But if the analysis indicates that in the depths of our soul is a sphere outside time and space—or more precisely, that it is our soul which belongs to this sphere—then consequently no death exists for our soul, because death is tied to both time and space. Therefore, the important thing is not whether the physical life is lost, but rather how it is lost. This is to say that the most important thing is whether or not man faced death having followed the inner voice in his life or not having followed it. Thus if Tolstoy is correct in saying that death itself is not frightening, but rather the whole lifetime before death, then perhaps in this is the essential difference between the death of a righteous person and that of a sinner.

There is indeed an enormous difference between the suffering of the imprisoned Solzhenitsyn, who on numerous occasions experienced moments of profound happiness in prison,[64] and the suffering of a typical Soviet engineer, who did not attain a "higher scope," i.e., who was completely deaf to the inner voice and the invisible spiritual world. Prior to imprisonment, therefore, he took everything from life which was at his command without the slightest sense of conscience. And now he was experiencing a terrible agony from the realization of the complete loss of everything by which he had lived.[65] "But there is only one life," the engineer said. Yes, only one life, but for what purpose is it given to us? Solzhenitsyn was both agreeing and posing a question.[66]

And perhaps for some, death is an exit into freedom, to use the expression of Tertz, while for others imprisonment is "perpetual exile," as Solzhenitsyn calls it in *Cancer Ward*. If this is the case, then it is entirely clear that a person may experience great joy even after being sentenced to death, as, for example, in an incident described by Solzhenitsyn: In this case, a woman had experienced the brightest week of her life after being sentenced to death[67]

One recalls that this same ecstasy and distinct sensing of the soul's immortality prior to execution was experienced by a revolutionary named Musya, who fearlessly followed her inner voice—as related by Leonid Andreev in his famous story, "The Seven That Were Hanged."

Notwithstanding the experienced inner happiness, do not both death and suffering of the destruction of the body still exist even for a righteous person? However, we know nothing about what awaits man behind the gates of death, and all that is left for us to do is speculate by using the analogy of prison confinement. And would it not be correct that if a human being were absolutely sinless—i.e., possessed such spiritual strength throughout his life from the moment of birth so as to follow only the spiritual voice within him—there would be no death whatsoever, since the physical laws would then be subject to him? We do not know anything for certain about this; however, it is indisputable that the immortality of the human soul becomes a self-evident fact for almost all people who survived the frightening experience of being close to physical destruction.

At the same time, under conditions of maximum loss of freedom, those who not only yielded, but even openly stood up for evil, also survived. However, what do we know about their final end?

KARMA

Faith in the immortality of the soul, which was achieved through suffering, and the acknowledgment through experience that everything that befalls man is fully deserved and that there are none who suffer without having committed a transgression, led the prisoners to the thinking held in the ancient teachings about Karma. This mystical precept asserts that a person will pay for every evil deed committed by means of this evil sooner or later befalling him. However, since a person may not always pay for his sins in the span of one lifetime, the tenets of Karma are bound to a belief in reincarnation, the embodiment of the human soul, asserting that through misfortunes in his present life, a person is paying for the sins he had committed in a previous life.

Christianity does not acknowledge reincarnation of the soul, and takes the stand that atonement for the sins committed in a single life awaits the person at the Great Judgment.

I would like to emphasize that the precept of Karma need not be inherently bound to the reincarnation of the soul. Precisely the fact that it is not known what a person experiences during the fearful hour of death may suggest that—even though there is no physical indication of atonement during the one lifetime—this atonement may nevertheless have occurred in this lifetime. In that sphere in which the human soul is situated there is no time, and hence Leo Tolstoy's Ivan Ilych was living through just this eternal agony.

One way or another, our authors were led to an understanding of Karma through life itself. Shifrin writes about how the realization of the tenets of Karma and reincarnation can change the entire human thinking process.[68] Solzhenitsyn describes his meeting with Doctor Kornfeld, who related to him one day prior to his death his certainty that everything which befalls man is fully deserved, occurring by means of a Karmic force.[69] Also in *Gulag*, Solzhenitsyn tells of an old woman who was absolutely certain that she would be liberated when God ruled that she had suffered enough for her sins—despite any adjudication or the ruled length of her confinement.[70] "God knows the term," said the old woman, and Solzhenitsyn attests that she did not write appeals or complaints to anyone. After a certain time lapse, an order arrived from Moscow and she was freed.

Through such experiences, the prisoners developed a sense of certainty that it is a mistake to try to achieve something by one's own will. What one should do is resign oneself to fate, and follow only the inner voice. And if an inner peace verifies the fact that man is following the inner voice even during times when he is inactive, when he endures and only waits for the moment to arrive, as in the case of the old woman, then everything will end in the best possible manner.[71] In fact, through attempts at willful interference in the flow of fate, man may only complicate and destroy his life.

And if suffering released one from transgression and, in the final analysis, at a specific moment led one out of captivity, then it was precisely the transgression which led one into prison. "We deserved everything which was to follow," writes Solzhenitsyn, and again, "everyone sees how he has been hurt, but does not see how he is guilty." And on numerous occasions he repeats that weakness submits one into the power of the NKVD, and that everything results because of fear.[72]

And here is an interesting paradox, which was observed by Grossman: Those prisoners who indeed fought and resisted the totalitarian regime prior to their arrest (in other words, followed a spiritual compass), considered that all prisoners were innocent. And conversely, those people who were innocent before the authorities, but were incarcerated nevertheless, considered that some sort of error had been made regarding them only, and that the others were indeed guilty.[73] And it was only suffering which opened their spiritual eyes to an understanding that indeed not many people were guilty before the authorities. However, they were guilty precisely before their own souls, because submission to fate does not mean submission before the rulers of this earth, but only to the demands of the soul itself.

For this reason, one cannot agree to inner slavery, even if only temporarily for the purpose of deceiving the evil forces and preserving one's own life. One may not, using Solzhenitsyn's words, "live, in order to live."[74] Man cannot avoid paying a penalty for this. For nothing in life happens by chance: both the bad and good, that which appears as a stroke of luck, or misfortune, are fully deserved. Deep inside the soul, which exists in a sphere outside of time, man knows in advance what will happen to him, even though only especially gifted seers realize this knowledge. Tertz, reflecting on this, recalls Plato's *anamnesis*, while Shifrin writes about Karma.[75]

However, is Karma synonymous with the fundamental law

or mysticism about which we talked above? No. Karma (or fate, which is the same thing) is the retribution for the deviation from following the spiritual compass, which happens only in the life of nonfreedom—more precisely, Karma is nonfreedom. The fundamental mystical law, on the contrary, brings out that freedom which is inexplicable to man's present mind—in which even the physical laws of the external world serve in the realization of man's striving when this striving is synonymous with the inner voice of the soul.

CONCLUSION

"How can one who is not spiritually free be liberated?" asks the author of *Gulag*, [76] and as though replying to this, Shifrin writes, "Only that one who will abandon the desert of spiritual slavery will become free."[77]

Spiritual slavery leads one to prison, spiritual freedom liberates one. For suffering opens man's eyes to the inner spiritual world, to the mystical compass, which is found in every man's soul, and to the offenses committed prior to the arrest. And as already mentioned, no one is to escape arrest or prison. And perhaps the greatest punishment is specifically when man does not undergo suffering during his lifetime, but is placed directly into "prison" for eternity when he dies.

We do not know anything for certain about this. One way or another, those who have undergone the anguish of maximum nonfreedom agree that a person, while in prison, saw himself as though through a magnifying glass, and experienced the most meaningful moments of his lifetime, to use Solzhenitsyn's words.[78] And Tertz corroborates this, saying, "A person while in prison is the most complete person."[79] Like Shifrin, Solzhenitsyn testifies that in the prison both he and others simultaneously passed through the process of corruption and ascent, a movement of goodness within the soul began, the person grew more tolerant and patient; in other words, after undergoing suffering a person began to become good.[80] Solzhenitsyn writes that all prisoners are individualities, that people in prison ennoble themselves and develop into interesting human beings, that the strongest love exists in prison camps.[81]

In contrast to the life of freedom perceived by people who are not imprisoned, who do not understand the most important questions facing man (sin, slavery, suffering, freedom, death) and hence live as though in a dream, prison life appears as the only real life, with the occupants being awakened from the dream. "I want to return to my fatherland, to my Archipelago," exclaims Solzhenitsyn,[82] while Tertz makes a paradoxical assertion that prison camp is the maximum freedom.[83]

Suffering had unlocked the way to true freedom, liberating man from everything external and superfluous in life . . . most significantly, from service and veneration of the idol of worldly power, because as the analysis had shown, all these idols were powerless to save man during the hour of his death. "Spiritual slavery is finished, once and for all," declares Solzhenitsyn,[84] and he blesses the prison.[85]

The experience in captivity has convincingly shown that enormous potential for concrete achievement of maximum freedom, as well as powerful forces for the transformation of the external world on the basis of mystical law, are contained in each human being. It was empirically asserted that the fate and life of every human being depend not on the authority of the worldly rulers, nor on external physical forces, but only on a mystical force—which for centuries was named God. The relation of this force to man appears to be defined only through the relation of man to the inner voice of his soul.

In essence, this is a triumphant confirmation of the ontological and empirical freedom of every individual human being. It is doubtful that there is anything more optimistic in this world than the realization that it is possible to influence world events in a concrete way—in opposition to the powerful forces of evil—by heeding only the liberating inner voice of the soul. And no outside forces can take away this freedom—his soul—from man. Only man himself can alter it.

Once again, the spiritual world becomes a visible reality. The comprehension of this experience cannot avoid changing the whole thinking process of humanity, of all the sciences and ideologies, of all the conscious life of our times.

Nevertheless, there is no absolute certainty in the fact that what was experienced is clearly understandable. Even though the authors who underwent the experience of captivity testify that man is freed only by following the inner compass, that this is the only route by which freedom can be achieved, the authors of these extraordinary books begin to generalize their experiences and start preaching to the people. And in their declarations it appears as though they do not believe that what preserved them will also save others.

Thus it appears that it is not the inner voice, but something external which should free man and lead humanity to a life of freedom. In Solzhenitsyn's view, it is a benevolent authoritarian rule, ideologically based on Eastern Orthodoxy. Panin places his hopes in the church and the classical church organization. Shifrin, it appears, counts on man to assimilate various esoteric doctrines and teachings.

Their own experience indicates just the reverse. No external organization of society, neither the church nor any ideology, nor esoteric or exoteric teachings, save man, nor do they liberate him. Only one mighty force, which rules both the mortal and material world, saves: the following of the inner voice frees man, perhaps even at the gates of death, as with Daniel amongst the lions.

There is none, and there never will be a substantive guarantee given either by reason, or by science, or by the church, or any other teachings regarding the inner voice—which is different for each individual. And there is no need for any guarantees or teachings for a person whose spiritual eyes were opened, in the same way as it is completely unnecessary to study where north or south will be in relation to where we will be tomorrow or the next day if we have a magnetic compass in our possession.

To use the words of Lev Shestov, "Only that one who does not know where he is going will reach the promised land."

September 1974

NOTES

1. Lev Shestov, *The Power of the Keys—Potestas Clavium* (Berlin: Skify 1923), p. 273.

2. A. Solzhenitsyn, *The Gulag Archipelago*, Vols. I-II (Paris: YMCA Press 1973-74).

3. A. Shifrin, *In the Fourth Dimension* (Frankfurt-on-Main: Posev, 1973).

4. D. Panin, *Notes of Sologdin* (Frankfurt-on-Main: Posev, 1973).

5. A. Tertz, *Voice from the Crowd* (London: Stenvalli, 1973).

6. Vasily Grossman, *Forever Flowing* (Frankfurt-on-Main: Posev, 1970).

7. *Gulag* II, pp. 587-89, Panin, p. 498.

8. Shifrin, p. 327.

9. Panin, p. 129.

10. Tertz, p. 102.

11. Tertz, p. 89.

12. Panin, pp. 137, 271.

13. Shifrin, p. 329.

14. Grossman, p. 118.

15. Tertz, p. 178.

16. *Gulag* II, p. 304.

17. *Gulag* I, p. 455.

18. *Gulag* II, p. 605.

19. Panin, p. 332.
20. Tertz, p. 271.
21. *Gulag* II, pp. 302-303.
22. *Gulag* I, pp. 139, 512-13, 541.
23. *Gulag* I, p. 117.
24. Panin, p. 336.
25. *Gulag* II, p. 595.
26. Panin, p. 389.
27. *Gulag* II, pp. 589-91, 597, 612.
28. Panin, pp. 259, 422-23, 436, 439, 443.
29. *Gulag* I, p. 17.
30. *Gulag* I, p. 482.
31. Panin, pp. 264, 266, 324, 442.
32. Panin, pp. 135, 229, 244, 307, 407, 489.
33. Shifrin, pp. 236, 245, 257, 272, 307, 346, 376.
34. Shifrin, pp. 190, 192.
35. Shifrin, p. 281.
36. Tertz, p. 97.
37. Panin, p. 257.
38. Panin, pp. 245-48.
39. *Gulag* I, p. 209.
40. Panin, pp. 91-3.
41. *Gulag* II, p. 469.
42. *Gulag* II, p. 367.
43. *Gulag* I, pp. 193-94.
44. Shifrin, pp. 50, 139.
45. Panin, p. 252.
46. *Gulag* II, p. 586.
47. Panin, p. 38.
48. Panin, p. 121.
49. *Gulag* II, p. 398.
50. *Gulag* I, p. 279.
51. Shifrin, p. 419.
52. Tertz, p. 193.
53. Shifrin, p. 182.
54. Shifrin, pp. 178-79.
55. Shifrin, pp. 447.
56. *Gulag* I, p. 368.
57. *Gulag* I, p. 484.
58. Shifrin, p. 403.
59. *Gulag* II, pp. 242-43.

60. *Zarubezhe* #39-40, Munich, 1973.
61. Ibid., article by Vera Pirozhkova, "Afterword."
62. G. Mayer, *Light in the Night* (Frankfurt-on-Main: Posev, 1967).
63. M. M. Bakhtin, *Problems in Dostoyevsky's Writings* (Leningrad: Priboi, 1929).
64. *Gulag* I, p. 593.
65. *Gulag* I, p. 208.
66. *Gulag* I, p. 275.
67. *Gulag* II, p. 645.
68. Shifrin, p. 194.
69. *Gulag* II, pp. 600-601.
70. *Gulag* II, pp. 610-11.
71. *Gulag* I, p. 554; II, p. 488.
72. *Gulag* I, p. 69; II, pp. 274, 322, 349.
73. Grossman, p. 92.
74. *Gulag* I, p. 287.
75. Tertz, p. 162.
76. *Gulag* II, p. 594.
77. Shifrin, p. 238.
78. *Gulag* I, p. 209.
79. Tertz, p. 273.
80. *Gulag* II, pp. 267, 598-99, 602-603, 614.
81. *Gulag* II, pp. 233-34, 606, 610, 618.
82. *Gulag* I, pp. 586-87.
83. Tertz, p. 279.
84. *Gulag* II, p. 501.
85. *Gulag* II, p. 604.

A Selected Bibliography
of Mihajlo Mihajlov's Work

Books

Moscow Summer

English Edition:	New York: Farrar, Straus and Giroux, 1965.
	London: Sidgwick & Jackson, 1966.
German Edition:	*Moskauer Sommer*. Bern: Schweizerisches Ost-Institut, 1965.
Dutch Edition:	*Gesprekken met Moderne Russische schrijvers.*
	Baarn: Het Wereldvenster, 1966.
Italian Edition:	*Estate a Mosca 1964*. Roma: Volpe Giovanni
	Editore, 1966.
Swedish Edition:	*Sommar i Moskva*. Stockholm: Allbert Bonnier
	Forlag, 1966.
Hindi Edition:	Delhi: National Academy, 1967.
Russian Edition:	Frankfurt/Main: Possev-Verlag, 1967.
	(First appeared in shortened form in Paris in 1965.)
Spanish Edition:	*Verano en Moscu*. Barcelona: Luis de Caralt, Editor, 1968.
Japanese Edition:	Tokyo: Keisho Shobo, 1974.

Russian Themes

Polish Edition:	*Tematy Rosyjskie*. Paris: Institut Literacki, 1966.

English Edition:	New York: Farrar, Straus and Giroux, 1968.
	London: MacDonald & Co., Ltd., 1968.
German Edition:	*Russische Themen.* Berne: Verlag Schweizerisches Ost-Institut, 1969.
Japanese Edition:	Tokyo: Kinokuniya Shoten, 1971.
Italian Edition:	*La fuga dalla provetta.* Milano: Arnoldo Mondadori Editore, 1971.

Flight From the Test Tube

| Russian Edition: | *Begstvo iz retorty.*Frankfurt/Main: Possev-Verlag, 1969. |

Pamphlets

Discussion about Theory of Alienation with Mr. Djilas

| Russian Edition: | Frankfurt/Main: Possev-Verlag, 1972. |
| Serbo-Croatian Edition: | London: Nasa Rec, 1972. |

Political Articles

In Serbo-Croatian:	Frankfurt/Main: Possev-Verlag, 1966.
	London: Savez Oslobodjenje, 1966.
In English:	"Memorandum." New York: Freedom House, 1966.

A Short Biography

Mihajlo Mihajlov was born in the town of Pancevo, not far from Belgrade, on September 26, 1934. His parents were Russian emigrés who in their youth arrived in Yugoslavia—his father was seventeen, while his mother was seven years old—after the civil war in Russia.

Mihajlov completed his high-school education in Sarajevo in Bosnia. Then he studied comparative literature at the Philology Faculty of Belgrade University, as well as at the Philosophy Faculty of Zagreb University, where he completed his degree in 1959.

After his army service, Mihajlov lived in Zagreb where he worked as a translator and published numerous articles in Yugoslav newspapers and periodicals. He also wrote for the Yugoslav radio. During this period he became well known as a specialist in modern Russian literature, a translator of Russian, and a public lecturer. In December 1963 Mihajlov was elected an assistant professor of the Department of Russian Literature and Language of the Philosophy Faculty of the Zadar Branch of Zagreb University.

In Zadar, Mihajlov taught Russian literature and prepared his doctoral dissertation. However, all of this was cut short by a term in jail for political reasons. During the summer of 1964 Mihajlov had spent five weeks in Moscow and Leningrad as part of the Cultural Exchange between Yugoslavia and the Soviet Union, and upon his return wrote a series of articles concerning his meetings with modern Russian writers— Erenburg, Leonov, Voznesensky, Akhmadulina, Okudzhava, and others—which were published in the literary periodical *Delo* in Belgrade in early 1965. However, after the publication of the second sequence of his articles, in March 1965, thanks to the pressure of the Soviet ambassador, President Tito criticized the periodical *Delo* and Mihajlov was promptly arrested and fired from the university faculty.

Since, by this time, his *Moscow Summer* had appeared as a book in some ten languages, including Hindi, and since many of his articles had appeared in the international press, his attempt to publish an independent socialist periodical, which would have been quite in accordance with the letter of Yugoslav law, received marked support from public opinion.

Unfortunately, the Yugoslav government preferred to follow the unwritten law of all one-party regimes, arrested Mihajlov with his friends, accused him of "hostile propaganda" and sentenced him first in Zadar in September 1966, later in April 1967 in Belgrade, whereas his friends were released after several months of investigation. Mihajlov was sentenced to three and a half years of strict regime jail and was barred for four years from the Yugoslav press, radio, and television after the completion of this sentence.

During his years in prison, his friends published in the West and translated into several languages his second book *Russian Themes*.

Until his arrest in October 1974, Mihajlov was living in Novi Sad, near Belgrade, working on his third book *Non-Scientific Thoughts* which he began during his earlier term. At the same time, he was planning to defend his doctoral dissertation "Motivation in Dostoyevsky's Novels." He is working also on a book on Samizdat entitled "Encounters With Live Books."

In February 1975 Mihajlov was tried for disseminating "hostile propaganda" about the Tito regime and was sentenced to seven years in prison.